BRAINSTYLES

Be Who You *Really* Are

YOU <u>CAN'T</u> CHANGE THE WAY YOUR BRAIN WORKS.

YOU <u>CAN</u> CHANGE THE WAY YOU USE IT.

By David Cherry and Marlane Miller

First Edition
#1588/ 1650

Published by BrainStyles, Inc., Dallas, Texas

BRAINSTYLES

Be Who You *Really* Are

copyright 1992 by David Cherry and Marlane Miller

Published by BrainStyles, Inc., Dallas, Texas

15851 Dallas Parkway, L.B. 140
Dallas, Texas 75248 - 6611

Library of Congress Number 92-082814

ISBN 0-9634406-0-8

CONTENTS

I

Reactions by Executives Who Use *The BrainStyles System*™

"Working with my group on the four brainstyles was invaluable. In addition to being an excellent source of self-insight, it also provided great insight into others. Understanding this enabled me to capitalize on their strengths and minimize their weaknesses. Projects and work teams could then be assigned to take advantage of these synergies and maximize results."

Guy M. Marsala,
Vice President, Sales, Pepsi Cola

"Every business person, salesman, and manager should have a good understanding of this material and its application to their work."

Steve M. Suddeth,
Principal, CM Financial, an Affiliate
of the Connecticut Mutual Alliance Insurance Company

"This is a whole system for living. I use it with my family, friends, and people at work. Knowing styles has made me more secure with people."

Dan J. Carrithers,
Product Manager, The Dexter Corporation

"Of all the seminars I have taken, BrainStyles has made the biggest difference in my life."

Director, Alcatel Network Systems,

"Learning about brainstyles has helped me learn about myself. I utilize my knowledge of different styles to manage myself as well as to understand other people's behavior. For me, understanding and anticipating how other styles operate has eliminated a lot of stress from my life."

Linda Foxworthy Sibilsky,
Controller, Plastics Division, The Dexter Corporation

"Becoming aware of my strengths empowers me to do what I do well, and not to spend time trying to become something I'm not. This has been very powerful for me and my relationships with and expectations for other people."

Steve Trozinski,
Distribution Manager, Pepsi Cola East

"I have studied and worked with entrepreneurs for more than 20 years. Isolating fundamental traits of successful entrepreneurs is a challenge. The potential of BrainStyles to help identify a successful entrepreneurial profile is exciting and will contribute to a breakthrough in our understanding."

Jerry F. White, Director,
The Caruth Institute of Owner — Managed Business,
Southern Methodist University, Dallas, Texas

Acknowledgements

Over the four years it took to produce this book, there have been many who listened and many who actively contributed. We sincerely hope that we give back as much as you gave. Here are a few:

Jane Albritton, a talented and professional writer in Dallas, first took this material from concept and vague observations to the page with style. Her organization and insights into what was really meant helped enormously in focusing both the authors. Her skill and intelligence as a writer are the bedrock of the writing here.

Avery Hunt Myers, our first agent, added skillful and insightful critique for logo, structure, and marketing, along with a lot of personal enthusiasm and referrals.

John Cox, who wrote the first draft of *In Search of Excellence*, edited us into a real book and was always there when needed.

Gary Weihs, a tireless, persistent friend and client gave enormously of his own blood, sweat and wins with real world tests of initial theories. Always willing to read and assess, he has been a major supporter.

Edie Lycke, a literate and endlessly supportive friend has consistently helped the production of this work over the never-ending hurdles, with discussion, review, and much-appreciated kind words.

Gene Landes did the research to uncover most of the technical resources at SMU's libraries in the midst of her own Ph. D.

Lee Ballard, principal of *The Naming Center*, not only came up with the rationale, he came up with the names of the four brainstyles — as well as the word *brainstyle*. Plus he added a much needed appreciation of the material.

Greg and Gary Miller, two brothers whose support and intelligent critique gave informed direction and insights for organization and rewrites.

Dr. Lawrence Peters, of the Neeley Business School of Texas Christian University helped design and test *The BrainStyles Inventory* with dedication and professionalism. His personal insights and support made working with him a treat as well as enhancing both the book and the *Inventory*.

Frank Campbell and Sandy Alberts were invaluable as editors and test cases whose insights have made a real difference. Steve Suddeth gave of time and thought. Steve Trozinski was very rewarding to work with. Ed Dalheim, publicist and enthusiast, Lloyd Ward, Don Tate — what a listener!

Thank you <u>all</u> for your patience and interest.

About the authors

The authors, entrepreneur and former CIBA-Geigy top executive David J. Cherry and corporate consultant Marlane Miller, are a husband/wife team who have been putting their concept of brainstyles to good use in the corporate arena, as well as in their personal lives, for over 14 years. Mr. Cherry, a chemical engineer by training, built and recently sold a sixty-million dollar business, having used brainstyles to determine the best combination of people to build a winning corporate team. He is now president and CEO of several companies and uses brainstyles to staff and operate them. Ms. Miller, with over 25 years of professional experience in corporate human resource development and human relations, is a frequent speaker at business forums and has built a broad corporate client base throughout the U.S., from PepsiCo, Northern Telecom and Kodak to Rockwell and Proctor and Gamble. She has been teaching The BrainStyles System™ to enthusiastic corporate audiences for several years.

At the age of 53, **David Cherry** sold his high-growth specialty plastics business (Dustin Hoffman was wrong; you can make it in plastics), to a Fortune 200 company and turned his 30 years' career into great personal wealth. He attributes his success to his breakthrough in developing and applying a model — the origin of *The BrainStyles System™*, for understanding and managing people. In part, this book is based on his experiences in coping with the most difficult business and people-related situations.

Originally from a small town in Iowa, he graduated as a chemical engineer from Iowa State University in 1959 and joined Firestone Tire and Rubber. Even as a junior engineer, he considered himself one of the five major department decision-makers and acted accordingly. This did not endear him to his superiors. But his frustrating early experiences in making what he considered breakthrough decisions with no attendant recognition led him toward a lifelong examination of business behavior and a search for answers as to why different people perform and react in such different ways in decision-making business environments.

Unhappy within the confines of a corporate technical arena, after much soul-searching, he campaigned for a job in sales. CIBA-Geigy hired him as a sales representative in 1967, and by 1970 he was sales manager, creating new markets, using his technical background to devise new sales product combinations, and generally bending rules to develop new business. By 1978 he was named General Sales Manager with national sales and marketing responsibilities.

In 1980, he was asked to run a CIBA-Geigy subsidiary, Ren Plastics. By the next year, recognizing that the company potential was underutilized in its current corporate confines, he had put together a deal to buy it. In five years, he took the business from $5 million to $40 million in sales, breaking into new markets and achieving patents in new product areas along the way. Since this book project began, he has started and invested in three diverse businesses which are also growing rapidly. Developing and applying the concepts reported in this book, David is a visionary practitioner and business leader. Now when David Cherry talks about business and business *BrainStyles*, he has results to back up what he says.

Marlane Miller, President of BrainStyles, Inc./Miller Consulting Services, has been a professional in the human development field since 1965. Working in the public sector as a training director, organization consultant and teacher, she entered private industry in 1976. In a multinational corporate setting, she created and delivered management development seminars for hundreds of executives, specializing in Team Building as a strategy to improve productivity.

She also developed expertise in fostering corporate-wide cultural change, and initiated a major four-year project to that end, involving more than 400 senior executives.

A graduate of UCLA, her specialty has been in evaluating and applying leading edge concepts that impact peoples' productivity and self esteem. This book is, in part, a logical extension of her years of experiences in the corporate training environment and as a private consultant.

She and David Cherry have created *The BrainStyles System*™ to help people understand and thus change the way they manage their work, their careers, their businesses and, in fact, their lives. She continues to write and make presentations on issues of corporate cultural change and how to be politically powerful. She also speaks, consults and trains managers and executives throughout corporate America about *BrainStyles*™ in a number of business applications, from general management skills to personal effectiveness.

Among her clients are PepsiCo, Kodak, Northern Telecom, Lone Star Gas, Proctor & Gamble, major restaurant chains, law firms and manufacturing operations. She has also served as a human resources consultant for such non-profit organizations as The United Way, Junior Achievement and the Dallas Women's Foundation.

Marlane has spent the last four years writing and researching, this book in consultation with David Cherry.

Preface

How Brainstyles Came To Be

In 1978, one of the authors, David Cherry, attended a popular and very effective seminar called "Managing Interpersonal Relationships" based on the work of industrial psychologist David Merrill who proposed a system for recognizing and typing people's actions into four "social style" categories. (See Appendix A). David returned to work, highly excited by the possibilities he envisioned for application of the social style principles, and began to discuss and apply them at work.

By 1979, both authors were testing the notions of behavioral styles and discussing their observations on a continual basis. Marlane Miller, in her work as a human resources professional, taught and assessed several style systems with a wide variety of managers. David applied social styles to teams and personal inter-actions in the business he led. Both were reading widely in a num-ber of fields related to business — psychology, science, organiza-tional behavior and management among them. Over the next few years David created a new approach for working with people. Marlane continued to gather new information, apply, test, and write about these new ideas as they were developed in discussion with David. What he arrived at was a breakthrough into a new theory and set of principles. Here are some of the mileposts in a process that continues today.

Meetings: A Perfect Laboratory

Company management team meetings were a perfect forum for David to observe behavior of the four different behavioral styles. In these meetings an interesting pattern began to emerge which couldn't be explained by observing outward behavior. One member of a management team who fit the behavioral description of an "analytical" type according to the social styles system, was predict-ed to be a lower assertive, less emotional person than his colleagues. Nonetheless, he was observed to be very assertive — even disruptive — in meetings, and then to be very methodical at other times. As issues were tracked for the team on a blackboard, he would ask questions and insist on returning to a topic that had been discussed ten to fifteen minutes earlier. A pattern began to emerge that had to do with *timing*: He was most disruptive when others had moved faster through a subject than he. It had nothing to do with his intelligence. He was one of the "brightest" members of the team; that is, he had amazingly accurate recall of facts and information. But much of his behavior did not seem to fit his behavioral style description. He acted assertively — even emotionally — to slow down meetings where *new topics* were discussed. The explanation that he might be a "combination of styles" (according to Merrill's work) seemed to force changing the basics. It led to contradictions in who a person was — and confused how to deal with them. David looked elsewhere for an explanation. Over a period of months and many discussions, it seemed that the real purpose of the analytical member's interruptions was to return to previously discussed subjects. Neither "social styles" nor other logical explanations explained why he did this. His good intentions were stated several times. He was not being disruptive just for the sake of it. He had genuine questions. The fact that he was known to be very intelligent seemed to contradict his apparent attempts to slow things down in meetings. He seemed to work according to his own inner speed or timing.

This led to a further observation: different members of the management team each had a different speed for addressing topics. And the speed varied consistently, according to a recognizable pattern.

Another manager in the company was behaviorally typed as a highly assertive, emotionally controlled individual (he showed little feeling). In dealing with his behaviors, people found that nothing they could say would threaten him. Confrontations seemed to have no effect at all. Yet two days after the manager had been confronted by a highly emotional employee he revealed that he *had* felt threatened — *but not until later.* Furthermore, when this same manager discussed any past emotional situations, he would either share or experience the feelings about the past as he was talking about it in the present. He did feel things, but on a *delayed* basis. *Time* seemed particularly important, again.

About this time (1982) the authors became familiar with material on left- and right-brain research. David posed several working hypotheses about brain interaction, genetics, and how to apply the ideas in a business setting. Supportive material became available with further study, all very recent scientific breakthroughs. (See Appendix A)

The differing functions of the two hemispheres of the brain when applied to create the four categories of behavior clarified the basis for four categories of thinking or processing styles, some of which seems to overlap with the behavioral styles. The work of the geneticists in the last decade have substantiated why months of counseling, rewards, and all the time-honored methods of getting someone to modify their behavior had little or no impact. Both of the authors, working with teams, watched heartfelt agreements fail that were made between team members. The agreements, based on any of several behavioral "styles" or "types" systems, depended on modifying or "flexing" individual behavior to *adapt* to another's expectations. The old saying "you can't change people" developed a much more profound meaning. BrainStyles as a philosophy was forming by addressing what others were not.

Finally, in applying a behavioral approach to assessing people's styles or predicting their strengths, some rather large mistakes were made in hiring *new* people. The cues that people gave in interviews and *even over a period of a few months* turned out to be behaviors they had *learned* to do, but, when pressed, were not their *real strengths*.

A technically competent, highly qualified, and seemingly assertive young man was hired to take over manufacturing. He talked of long term plans, he talked of people and how to develop them. In meetings he laughed often and looked others in the eye. He was, according to the behavioral system, a typical "expressive type:

outgoing, enthusiastic, persuasive, fun loving, spontaneous."[1] But after a few months, plans were not implemented. There was a line of supervisors outside the manufacturing manager's office. The new manager was attending to issues *one at a time*. He was approaching the job in a linear, detailed fashion. He was not delegating. He was controlling the information. His real strengths were exactly the opposite of his outward behavior. There was clearly a poor job fit for him; the expectations for him and what he could deliver were not aligned.

After this incident, a re-evaluation of the behavioral approach was begun to get at the causes for behavior, and what, if anything, could be counted on to reliably predict a person's strengths.

In the same year, 1982, the authors also began a self-study program called *A Course In Miracles*[2] which assists the reader in perceiving the world using one of two systems of thought: love or fear. One of the major objects of the *Course* is for the student to "teach only Love, for that is what you are." To do so requires reversing the rules and accepted perceptions of a world based on fear and judgment. It requires looking beyond appearances. It demands personal responsibility and self-love in order to open our unlimited spirits to be the best selves we can be. Applying these principles in business became the overriding (right-brained) philosophy for *The BrainStyles System™*. The left-brained, fact-based side describes the technology and mechanics of the genetic hardware of the physical brain which limits our abilities to be and do everything.

Knowing your strengths can be limiting (the fear) or they can be used as launching pads (the acceptance).

In dealing with hundreds of colleagues, friends, and clients, we have found that confronting this material involves releasing the ego's demand for perfection, its judgments and criticism to begin a natural process of self-acceptance. Self-acceptance is the bottom line of brainstyles. We offer this material as a beginning of a limitless process of personal empowerment through increased self-respect. This automatically results in respect for others, with increasing tolerance for true diversity of differences in the workplace — differences in ability that create a whole new culture for a family, a team or a business — based on what is natural.

A real difference in this book from others in the field stems from the fact that the philosophy and technology were originally developed and tested by a very successful businessman — not a psychologist or academic — who has *lived* and *successfully applied* these principles in his *own* workplace.

David Cherry headed up a specialty plastics firm based in Arlington, Texas from 1981 until 1986 when it was acquired by a Fortune 200 specialty chemical firm. The company was led from a financial disaster ($5 mm in annual sales with overall losses of $400,000 per year), 20 employees, inconsistent product quality, equipment failures, in a recession, with 24% interest rates, to an extraordinary market success in a mere five years:

- The company achieved and maintained a number one market position against increased competition from the US, Europe and Japan.
- The company received the "Q1 Award" from Ford Motors in 1986 as the outstanding quality supplier in its industry.
- Sales reached the $40,000,000.00 range.
- Employees numbered 200 in three locations.

However, as the employees themselves expressed, the things that counted in their workplace were how the company was led.

- People were motivated and performed very well because it was fine for everyone to have a different point of view. Everyone was encouraged to identify their strengths and work at the maximum in those areas.
- People made agreements based on what they personally could deliver.
- There was an absence of "politics" — that is, under-cover maneuvering to get resources or get on the good side of the boss. People were not engaged in figuring out what the boss

wanted. *Brainstyles* discussions meant open agendas. Everyone was included. The environment was very safe for all to speak up from their own point of view. David's role as chief was to provide the unifying vision and keep the teams on track.

This book is a guide to getting you started on the road to self-acceptance by focusing on who you are and letting go of who you're not. How and where you apply it is unlimited. We have seen companies, clients and friends grow and succeed by using the technology and applying these principles.

PART I: <u>WHY</u> KNOW THYSELF?

When communications fail,
when trying to change just makes things worse,
and you're sick of trying,
look inside to value
what's already
there.

Chapter One

It Works To Be Who You Are

Discovering the ways in which

you are exceptional,

the particular path

you are meant to follow,

is your business on this earth.

Bernie S. Siegel, M.D., surgeon and author

CHAPTER ONE

IT WORKS TO BE WHO YOU ARE

Do you have a mental list of what you need to improve? Do you have a *role model* — a secret image of the ideal you — someone who represents everything you're *not?* Have you spent most of your life trying to improve yourself?

"To become a leader, you must become yourself, become the maker of your own life," says professor Warren Bennis who wrote a book on leadership after studying 28 of America's most successful people. He poses a challenge for us to play life as a game that is "natural to play."[1] In a *Fortune* cover story in June, 1991 called "BrainPower," the leading statement tells us that "Intellectual capital is becoming corporate America's most valuable asset and can be its sharpest competitive weapon. The challenge is to **find what you have — and use it.**"[2] What happens to this wisdom in the daily course of doing business? Here's a typical example.

A top performing saleswoman who had won all the company contests for dollars earned reported that she had been promoted to corporate headquarters in Connecticut. She ran into trouble with her new boss immediately.

"I could walk into a new account and know in five minutes what the problems were and how our products could solve them. I'd talk it over with my boss and all he'd ask me for was documentation. He wanted the analysis, the facts. Word got to his boss that we weren't getting along. I was sent to a consultant who gave me a test — The Myers Briggs[3], I think. The consultant explained how I was more intuitive, my boss more analytical and factual. He told me that in order to get my point across I had to speak my boss's language. So, I went back, tried to get better at due diligence, make reports, analyze, and be factual. The more I tried, the more mistakes he found. I wasn't making sales. He wasn't happy. I quit."

Why This Book

To enable you to discover the answer to the most fundamental of questions: "Who are you?", and to do what is *natural* for you to do to live a highly productive and satisfying life is the purpose of this book. There is nothing available today that asks you to stop trying to change or improve yourself. This book will show you how to <u>be</u> <u>who</u> <u>you</u> <u>really</u> <u>are</u> and be it more effectively.

In the above example, the saleswoman, the boss and the organization lost and lost badly by telling someone to adapt to another's strengths; to try to focus on her weaknesses and change them. This will not work for her or for anyone.

Item: *Semantic abilities are genetically based.[4] Studies of six month-old infants show that a natural ability to learn language sounds is demonstrated by that age. Conclusion: there is a clear genetic basis for learning language.[5]*

Item: *Studies of identical twins with the same genetic material raised apart in different families soon after birth, are found to be 70-80% similar in aptitudes, intelligence, brain activity, values, and how outgoing they are. (See Appendix)*

Item: *Entrepreneurs think alike, no matter what country they call home. People who start businesses think they hold a different set of beliefs than the rest of society, whether their community is Taiwan or Texas, says a 13-nation study of 700 entrepreneurs by the Wharton School's entrepreneurial center... Entrepreneurs, for instance believe others are more likely to put off work than they are, the study says. Such egocentric views have long fostered tension in society, says Ian MacMillan, a Wharton professor and coauthor.[6]*

There is mounting evidence that our basic abilities, the cards we were dealt, are more defined than we would like to think.

Moreover, they determine who we become, whether we grow up in Taiwan or Texas. When people say "You must change to be successful," it is not only impossible, **it undermines who you are** naturally, and lessens what you might offer. And yet this faulty notion sends millions on wild goose chases in search of personal perfection. Personal growth and training seminars too often translate into learning to be someone you're not. Seminars are focused on shoring up weaknesses. By definition this sends a message to adapt and change who you are and what you do best. *Perfection requires being all things to all people.* The harvest of this approach is little productivity with no satisfaction, limited, short term success at trying to please others at the expense of lifelong accomplishment for yourself.

When Wendell was a boy his father told him that the only way to succeed was to "make it on your own." Wendell grew up on a farm and watched how hard work and solitary effort paid off. "This was the model of success, to me," Wendell reported twenty years later. Wendell had become a manufacturing manager — a successful one. And on the way up, he had worked hard to establish a reputation for a hard-working, results-oriented, bottom-line thinker. He attended several company workshops where his "social style" was assessed by his peers, as well as himself, to be a highly controlling, results-oriented style, (a "driver"). But there was a problem for Wendell. He was constantly getting feedback that he needed to learn to "control his emotions." He kept reacting to people and situations, instead of being the cool, logical guy his "social style" predicted. "They tell me I'm not a team player. And yet I really care about people — I even think that is what my <u>real</u> mission in life is, to develop people," he confided. After hearing the basic principles of brainstyles, he reported: "The **Time Zero** idea [how he reacts to *new* information] is what I can't get around. I <u>do</u> react emotionally first and think about it later. I've <u>learned</u> to work alone, and be tough. But I'm not sure this is *really me.*" Wendell, after eighteen years with his company, is considering some counseling to help sort through his questions about his real strengths so he can figure out what he really wants to do with the rest of his career. Brainstyles raised the central question of what is *natural* and what is *learned* for Wendell.

Where do you look to find the self that is you? The self that can say to everyone — including bosses — "Here I am, and here is what I do well. Exploit it, and I can contribute beyond your expectations." The quest for such self-awareness is as old as Socrates' pronouncement: "Know thyself." And we would add that, once you know it, **don't change it!** A rose is a rose is a rose. A rose can't be a gardenia.

This book will help you discover what your *brainstyle* is. We hope to get you started on a path of self-discovery in order to avoid the career crisis you will have to confront if you get promoted based on what you've learned rather than what is natural to you. It is difficult to discover our natural strengths because they are quite invisible to us. We take for granted what we do effortlessly and focus instead on what we need to *correct* — usually to live up to another's standards. This is often necessary (learning to get along in modern society) *up to a point.* That point comes when we lose the distinction between who we are and who we are trying to be to please others — when we are continually stretched finding answers that take too much effort and time and bring no joy to us in the search for them. When it's too much pain and not enough gain.

When you learn about brainstyles, you'll know why you approach things the way you do, and *why* other people are either *similar* or *different* — not *good* or *bad.* Understanding brainstyles will define what you do when you are at your best — how you learn, make decisions, deal with conflict — what your true gifts are. And once you understand your gifts, you can focus on building satisfaction and self-esteem by making choices within your abilities and interacting with others more successfully. This can help achieve better job fit and career selection. Personal relationships can be based on expectations that "you are different" rather than "you must be like me." The first will work. The second will <u>not</u>.

When Gary, a 29-year old plant manager, met with the

Operations Vice President in his company, it was not a pleasant experience for him. Gary was careful to assemble all the facts, assess the situation and prepare a report that thoroughly supported his request for a budget increase. His VP, an impatient, results-focused man, wanted a one-page summary starting with the "bottom line." Gary wanted to detail what was involved in his conclusions so the VP would understand better what the decision required. The VP got more impatient the more Gary explained. But after he learned about brainstyles, Gary tried a different tack. In a subsequent meeting, at which he was requesting a major expansion to his plant, Gary prepared a summary. He began explaining his request when the VP exploded "Damn it, Gary, just give me the punchline! You took an extra three days! What's the decision?" Gary looked at him and said, "You know, I'm never going to give you the decision you want as fast as you want it. You'll always be faster at that than I will. But I will tell you something: I will work as hard as I can and as fast as I can to make what I give you as accurate and as solid a decision as possible. It may take two days longer, but you can take it to the bank. And, he added, there's too many 'hip-shooters' around here. You need someone you can count on."

The VP sat down. He could tell Gary was not making an excuse for delays. It was the truth. He *was* accurate and thorough. Gary was saying what he could be counted on for, and that he could be counted on to deliver it to meet the VP's needs to the best of his ability. Gary was playing from strength. They both knew it.

They never had another meeting like that one again. The VP became one of Gary's strongest supporters in the organization, recommending him for several promotions in the next few years.

Natural Brainstyles vs. Learned Behavior

The American ethic of you-can-be-successful-if-you-work-hard-enough often slips us a curve. Underlying it is an assumption that there is a right way to do things (fit this model), a best way to behave (be like *him*), in order to get where you're going (where the author or speaker is). It's implied by all the measures and tests and lists of behaviors used as benchmarks for determining how far short of your potential you fall. They all reinforce the notion that who you *already are* is not good enough. The challenge of brainstyles is simple but not easy: Be who you are and negotiate with another to reach agreements <u>without</u> changing <u>either</u> style.

The Brain and Our Perceptions

Whether we are aware of it or not, our actions toward others are, by necessity, based on incomplete assessments we make. This is because of the way our brain functions to gather and process information. We cannot handle all the available data. We organize it by *seeing what we have already decided to see.* "The eye ... transmits less than *one trillionth* of the information reaching its surface" brain researcher Robert Ornstein reports.[7] We relate to others with very limited perceptions, and no real system to find out **why** people act as they do. Therefore, we react out of habit rather than awareness.

Basic business systems such as Management by Objectives, human resource planning and career counseling are based on using observable behavior to make evaluations of people's performance, potential and progress. All these systems are based on one or both of the following assumptions: (1) **you can learn to change your behavior and become more competent** and (2) **you need to** focus on and **correct those behaviors that you can't do well now.** Both of these **assumptions are false, misleading and defeat** rather than develop **the person.**

This book, then, proposes a system for understanding and predicting individual strengths and interactions. It may sound familiar at times. We find that once you grasp and get familiar with the basics, you will have a new way to evaluate your potential, your gifts, and apply your "intelligence." Starting with the idea that you are just fine the way you are, this can be an empowering path to your own enrichment.

The BrainStyles System™

There are three critical factors underlying human behavior: How we take in information, how we process that information to reach conclusions, and how we express the information we have processed.

1. How we take in information.

Jung called this function "perceiving" or selecting out of the thousands of stimuli available what we literally pay attention to. What we know now is that our physical organs receive and transmit data to both the left side of the brain and the right side. Our brains pay attention to data in recognizable patterns from the left and right sides of the brain.[8]

2. How we process information into conclusions.

Conclusions are more than just opinions or reactions. A conclusion is the sorting of inputs, the elimination of some and choice of others to reach a decision. The processing of information depends on which side of the brain is dominant and at what speed it communicates across functions and through the *corpus callosum* from one side of the brain to the other.

3. How we express information.

People give out information (behave) the same way they took it in. We say, *as you file, so you retrieve.* In order to influence another, if you think about it, you must know how the other reaches conclusions. Whether someone is extroverted and assertive, or introverted and quiet, is certainly a visible and fascinating aspect of how people act. But it is only one determiner of how they think or what you can predict them to do. If you have a system for determining how the person handles *new* information, you will be able to predict the most basic component of what you trust them for: how they make decisions. And if you do so in the context that you are not asking them to change — you are not trying to manipulate them — you will be able to establish a system based on trust and mutual respect, the real basis for growth of any kind.

BrainStyles, Left and Right

How the brain processes new information is the key determiner of a person's *brainstyle. Brainstyle* describes how an individual carries out the three key factors in relating to the world: learning (taking in information), making decisions (processing information), and relating to others (expressing information).

There are four basic "brainstyles" created by the interaction and speed of the brain in processing input. But, first, let's briefly summarize what we have found out in the last 40 years about the brain and how it works.

Nobel laureate Roger Sperry conducted his brain research in the 1960's. His work with epileptics whose brain stems were severed in order to stop painful seizures demonstrated that the right and left hemispheres of the brain do business quite differently. Much further testing has been conducted by many scientists on normal people by recording the electrical impulses on the scalp to measure the location and intensity of brain activity. As Robert Ornstein found:

> By recording the tiny electrical potentials on the scalp, my colleagues and I could show that most people activated and suppressed their hemispheres, one at a time, when they were reading or drawing, thinking critically or creatively, reading technical material or stories. I characterized these two minds as rational and intuitive, the rational faculties depending predominantly upon left-hemisphere processes, the intuitive (immediate knowing of the environment) on the right.[9]

Further studies by Ornstein, Sperry, and neurophysiologists have established specific functions associated in general with different parts of the brain. What we are learning is that they are carried on *separately* in the brain itself and therefore must come together in our awareness in order for us to complete our thinking or make a decision. This takes *time*.

As we speak of left brain and right, these are the abilities associated with each side. Further research is finding there is more complexity in the brain than this. However, the metaphor of "left" and "right" still holds. (See Appendix for more detail.)

"Left" Brain Functions	"Right" Brain Functions
Speaking, verbal ability	Non-verbal, ability to understand meanings
Dealing with fine detail	Connecting details into a whole
Learns	Knows
Logical analysis	Intuition, insight, knowing
Linear, literal understanding of what is seen, felt, heard	Spatial, holistic abilities— understanding in three dimensions, a sense of direction.
Tends to project the past into the future	Imagination, daydreaming, envisioning the future
Mathematical analysis	Emotional awareness
Factual, concrete	Mystical, spiritual
Time and Measurement	No Time or Measures
Speaks, but cannot Know	*Knows, but cannot Speak*

The Four BrainStyles Defined

There are four basic patterns of brain interaction. Why only four? Hippocrates to Jung through all the modern psychologists continue to find four basic patterns in behavior. Our testing and observations substantiated the same number. Further, the distinctions between the four brainstyles based on our tests have gotten clearer the more people have tested them.

The work being done on the brain at the neural level suggests that this organ which, if it were a computer, would be a ten story building the size of Texas, is a vastly complex one. Surely, one would say, there must be more than four natural patterns that it could create. One could argue that there are probably some five billion patterns the brain creates — one for every person alive. The point is: What works? In testing a basic set of strengths for yourself, if you find that you fit one of the basic brainstyles and can use it in the way we suggest, you will maximize your potential along with everyone else's. You can move forward with clarity instead of confusion.

BrainStyles at Time Zero

Left brain, right brain. Logic, imagination. We *all draw from both sides of the brain, but not necessarily in the same order or at the same speed.* Our brainstyles are different, and those differences show up most vividly when we respond to a totally new situation. We call this new situation a "**Time Zero event.**" We identify a brainstyle by what happens in the brain at **Time Zero** — a time when our perception is *there were no other times like this.* When we perceive a situation as familiar, a Time Three or Five, we are drawing from experience or memory. For instance, if you are a student, you may consider a new test a **Time Zero** event. Actually, only the content of the test may be unfamiliar, and the decisions made to answer it will be mostly from memory. A **Time Zero** event or situation for a student is more apt to be taking an entirely new subject or, better yet, outside the classroom entirely, in a new life situation like a first job.

Time Zero Events

A **Time Zero** event is one where a decision about action to take is required. The internal perception is that *this is new to me* or *I'm not sure what to do.* A **Time Zero** is a subjective event. It is the time when you must process information in order to act on it.

Event	new	somewhat familiar	learned experience	
Time	0	1	2	3	4

Example: Coming to a new intersection with five intersecting streets, each person may perceive the situation in one of two ways — familiar or unfamiliar. When the person realizes internally that *I've seen this before*, a response is brought forward to take action from what has been *learned*. If the person does not see the situation as familiar, they will process the incoming information according to brainstyle. The speed will be faster (more automatic) when needing only to recall rather than process the information.

The Four BrainStyles

THE KNOWER

[to know: to perceive clearly and with certainty; to have fixed in the mind or memory]

The **KNOWER** is the brainstyle that operates out of the left brain at **Time Zero**. The name for this rapid left-brain response was picked for her/his self-described clarity and certainty very soon after being presented with new information. **The Knower** collects, processes, then delivers information primarily from the left side of the brain. This looks like a swift, linear, definite response that structures, evaluates, and focuses on the result or "bottom-line." Only later does the right brain introduce feeling or emotion to the left brain response — from minutes to several days after **Time Zero**. Competent **Knowers** bring a logical, factual clarity to complexity. If diagramming the communication between their hemispheres, it would look like this:

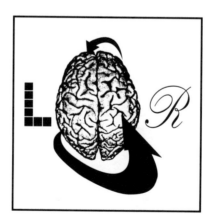

THE CONCEPTOR

[a concept: a general idea or notion formed by
combining all characteristics]

At **Time Zero** the **CONCEPTOR** processes information rapidly with both left- and right-brain resources. The **Conceptor** rapidly, and often randomly, goes from facts and logic to emotion and possibilities. He files information in categories according to his own logic and insights, and delivers generalities, overviews, or a combination of the data available. A left/right brain exchange happens instantaneously, as the information passes rapidly from left brain to right brain and back around again. At **Time Zero,** there appears to be random access of information because it is not stored in a linear fashion. Right-brained illogical connections are made among data that can promote rapid conceptual leaps, new ideas, or erratic behavior. The process often focuses on future possibilities. The **Conceptor** is hard to follow in new (or unrehearsed) situations because he or she is giving out broad information in a kind of personal shorthand — loaded words and ideas without details or explanation. The competent **Conceptor** brings a creative overview to complex or new situations.

Picturing the internal communication of the Conceptor's brain speed looks like this:

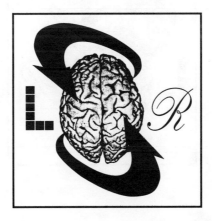

THE CONCILIATOR

[to conciliate: to overcome distrust or hostility;
placate; win over; to make compatible, reconcile]

At **Time Zero** the **CONCILIATOR** is a brainstyle dominated by the right brain. This brainstyle is so named because the first impulse of the right brain is to combine information, look for similarities, harmonize differences or bring together relationships. Unstated, non-verbal nuance is comfortable input for this brainstyle. The **Conciliator** can "read" people, body-language, and the unspoken dynamics in a group with an ease that is not as tempered by left-brain logic and analysis as would be the **Conceptor's,** or any other, brainstyle. At **Time Zero** the **Conciliator** accesses an immediate, emotional or intuitive response directly from the right brain. There is an instant awareness of a feeling response when a new subject is introduced. Immediate action is non-linear, feeling, and spontaneous. Later (from minutes to days later), left-brain measures and logic judge and organize the initial reaction. The competent **Conciliator** brings meanings and/or feelings to a situation that is beyond literal words, and brings the people together to get it done.

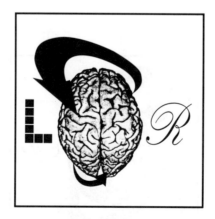

THE DELIBERATOR

[to deliberate: to weigh or consider; studied;
careful or slow in deciding]

At **Time Zero** the **DELIBERATOR** collects and assesses information. This brainstyle is gifted in not having much of a visible reaction immediately. This brainstyle offers a delayed, balanced response as the **Time Zero** stimulus prompts a search in memory or mental files where facts and feelings are stored. **Deliberators** are best at "filing" or remembering approximately the way the data were originally presented. In other words, the **Deliberator** is most capable of being neutral (if there is such a thing), factual, and objective. This includes addressing and discussing complexity — to get all the facts lined up as they were initially perceived. When this brainstyle sorts information it is organized by how it has been assessed against established standards — right or wrong, or compared to a *model* (a **Deliberator** favorite) that has been assessed as correct. Reaching a conclusion is a lengthy sorting process for the **Deliberator** — *unless it has been made previously,* or unless there is a learned process to *re-apply* to the new facts that can speed up the sorting. The exchange of retrieved information results in memory-based or experience-based, logical action. The competent **Deliberator** first brings reason and facts to a situation. Later (from seconds to hours) are added intuition or conclusions.

The picture of the **Deliberator** brainstyle speed at **Time Zero** looks like this:

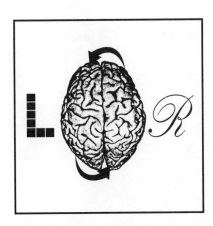

How The Brain Causes Behavior: A Summary

KNOWER at TIME ZERO:	CONCEPTOR at TIME ZERO:	CONCILIATOR at TIME ZERO:	DELIBERATOR at TIME ZERO:
Left Brain Reacts	Right-Left-Right Brain	Right Brain Reacts	Recalls What Is Stored
Logical, Structured response	Feeling + Logic Inconsistent response	Spontaneous Reaction	Reports Objectively or Asks Questions

KNOWER APPEARS	CONCEPTOR APPEARS	CONCILIATOR APPEARS	DELIBERATOR APPEARS
Cool, Factual, Structured, Decisive Focused	Creative, Passionate, Strong-Willed, Dynamic	Emotional, Responsive, Empathetic, Spontaneous	Thoughtful, Indifferent, Cautious, Even

KNOWER STRENGTHS	CONCEPTOR STRENGTHS	CONCILIATOR STRENGTHS	DELIBERATOR STRENGTHS
"Chunks" Information, Structures, Decides without emotion, Focus is on the results; Clearly defines new applications of existing ideas in the future	Concepts, Vision, Creating from nothing, Responding to change, Holistic analysis that begins as a general concept	People/Social Skills: "Reading" feelings, Accepting others, Projects with people imagination, Subjective analysis	Assessing, Creating from something, Improving, Planning, Executing the plan, Step by Step analysis

BrainStyles Principles

Our thesis is a simple and straightforward one which explains how the brain, behavior and time go together.

- *Your brain is your genetically determined "hardware" to process information and make decisions.*

Knowing this means knowing your limits — the key to becoming "the maker of your own life" as Professor Bennis asks us to do.

- *You do not choose how your brain functions. You choose how to apply what your brain naturally provides. Trying to do otherwise produces inner conflict and dissatisfaction.*

Choosing to be who you are is the definition of happiness.

- *The brain hemispheres, each performing different functions, communicate their information at different speeds in different people.*

Understanding how to time your own decisions and interactions is the foundation for win-win relationships — where you do not have to take things personally.

- *The speed of information exchange between the brain hemispheres manifests itself in four general patterns of behavior. This pattern is called a brainstyle.*

Separating brainstyles from behavior is the same process as making a friend — looking behind actions for real strengths. Using these principles means expanding the people you can be friends with. You <u>can</u> learn to strategize with rather than react to others. You can stop trying to get another to do what they don't want to do. You can start working with who they are already. It may take some time and exploration for both of you to uncover what each of your real strengths are.

- *A person's brainstyle can be determined by observing what happens in situations that are new to the person, where there are (or seem to the person to be) no prepared answers to the situation. These new situations we call <u>Time Zero</u> events. Responses to events after <u>Time Zero</u> involve "learned behavior," i. e., behavior in which a response has been tried out at least once. These learned behaviors are practiced ways* *of responding to situations. They can include behaviors natural to all four brainstyles.*

- *You cannot determine a person's brainstyle by observing learned behaviors.*

Where Jung and Myers-Briggs speak of "preferences" for mental functioning, it has become apparent that we can no more choose to process information differently at **Time Zero** than we can choose to do other physical functions differently. We can learn to compensate or improve something — run faster, speak more distinctly, retrieve the use of a damaged limb — but we cannot change the basic functioning of the "equipment" we have. Even if we choose to do so. And when we learn to improve a mental function outside our natural area of strength, it will never really produce the results or the satisfactions afforded by our natural gifts.

Determining Your BrainStyle

By now you have read enough perhaps to be curious about how to *determine your own brainstyle.* It is our experience that this is not easy for everyone. To figure out your brainstyle requires introspection and self-awareness that you may not practice regularly because you are focusing on what you do in your job. And your job may demand other strengths than your natural gifts. Moreover, others' feedback to you is filtered through their brainstyle, and may not be a very reliable source. Only patterns over time show real strengths. You need to combine feedback with insight and the brainstyle descriptions to get what is right for you.

Ed, a very competent public relations professional, has a very polished self image. "I think of myself as very organized and results-oriented." After several weeks of studying *brainstyles,* he said the real truth about his strengths was that "I'm a very responsive guy — the last person to talk to me, or the one who makes the biggest noise gets my attention. I work all the time at being organized and focused. But that's not my real strength. I would never have seen this without the new perspective of *brainstyles.*"

You need to *take some time* to think about the following

questions, read more of the descriptions in the chapters that follow, *and don't be fooled by learned behaviors.* A short method for determining your brainstyle follows. A 24 question *BrainStyle Inventory* is in Appendix B. You may wish to take it after reading the next chapter. It is a learning tool designed to help you determine your **Time Zero** strengths as well as your pattern of strengths — what you're best at — over time.

It takes practice to recognize *brainstyle.*

Determining Your BrainStyle: A Quick Look

1. Think of a time when you were confronted with some new information. You were in an unfamiliar situation. You recognized that "this is new" or "I'm not sure."

2. What was your immediate reaction — not what you said or did, but what you realized before that, inside — your thoughts or feelings?

3. Which of the following descriptions sounds like you at **Time Zero**?

(See Chapter 6)

I become analytical first. I look at the underlying issues, dissect the larger problem into smaller, more manageable parts, and then try to figure out how to handle those smaller problems. I rely on logic, facts, and my ability to think through issues. I do not decide too quickly on new issues. I am aware of emotions and intuition somewhat later, balancing them with facts.

(See Chapter 5)

My first response is usually a feeling one to novel or unusual problems. I seem to know what to do without much detailed analysis — I rely on my intuition in these situations. I usually come up with an idea, direction or more creative solution that just feels right to me at that time. Later I add facts or analysis. I am excellent at people-process and shorter-term problems.

(See Chapter 4)

I can react either emotionally or logically, deciding quickly. What I do that others don't is to capture the new issue or problem with a concept to give a direction. I can quickly frame a strategy for the long term. I may not share my feelings right away. I get to details later, and not very well. On balance, my strengths focus on inventing and developing ideas more than relationships.

(See Chapter 3)

At first I quickly sort information into topics or categories — not so many details. I may be abrupt. I tend to decide quickly what to do. Later I may be aware of my feelings about a topic. I am not as good with people as I am with applications and systems. I can quickly define practical solutions in the future to solve today's problems.

4. Think of similar situations. Is there a pattern to your response or reaction over a long period of time?

Chapter Two

**What Knowing About BrainStyle
Can Mean For You**

> "There is no struggle, no pain,
>
> no competition, and no comparison
>
> to others when being who I really am"

Louise L. Hay, author, counselor

CHAPTER TWO

WHAT KNOWING ABOUT BRAINSTYLE CAN MEAN FOR YOU

Understanding *brainstyles* means understanding your limits, appreciating them, and not competing in your *non-strengths* (the strengths of other brainstyles). It is terribly frustrating to want to be something other than you are. Having read this far, you understand that everyone's physical "equipment" has limits built in. Your spirit, however, does not. There is no limit to how much you can love or give of yourself. Nor is there any limit to the success you can achieve.

How your brain processes information at **Time Zero** determines how you make decisions. **Knowing how your brain takes you to a decision** — *and that others may take a different route on a different schedule* — **is the single most important piece of information you can have to be successful.** It is decisions and how people make them that you count on people for. When are they going to take action? Will they do what they say they will? The answers to these questions are the basis for how we *trust* one another.

Understanding how the brain works *and in what time frame* can tell you how you learn, how you process information, and how you relate to your environment. Educational systems, prizing memory of details, analysis and synthesis of facts, have not considered this information and primarily train people to be competent **Deliberators,** whether that is their brainstyle or not. As the new researchers are explaining, schools do not prepare us for work — or life, for that matter.[1] So career strategists have used the "adapt it - fix it - try it" model to prepare people to charm their way into jobs that don't fit. Interviews are designed to elicit learned behaviors that fit who interviewers want to see; interviewees tell them what they want to hear. Our institutions — education and business — need to be changed so that they are founded on the strengths of the people in them.

Learning: How BrainStyles Input Information

Have you ever noticed when someone cannot seem to understand something simple you're trying to say? It could be because of how they need to take in or input the information.

The four brainstyles split into two categories for learning or gathering information. The **Conceptor** and the **Knower** draw from, *but remain relatively independent of,* the environment around them. It stimulates their own internal computers — which then carry on without your input, thank you. This internal surety is often expressed as telling others the answers, or assertiveness. Assertiveness to less assertive people is judged as "aggressive," a label both these brainstyles are given by others. We sometimes call **Knowers** and **Conceptors** persecutors or villains. We label them arrogant, self-absorbed. We bristle at their criticism and admire their brilliance. We try to regulate their agendas. In our focus on their behavior, we lose sight of the gifts they bring. Steven Jobs, described in detail in the chapter on the **Conceptor**, is a classic case. Michael Meyer, the author of a book describing "The Dreams That Drive The Great Businessmen"[2], talks about his personal difficulties in dealing with the "visionary" Jobs: "Jobs didn't give a hoot whether I liked him or not. He only wanted my respect and my subservience. He wasn't interested in a 'relationship'. He wanted control."[3] Meyer continues with his perceptions (can you guess *his* brainstyle?) and the interpretations of Jobs' behavior by others: the descriptions include Jobs' "browbeating 'bozos' who don't measure up to his exacting standards", and his "almost willful lack of tact." It is only Meyers' thoroughness in describing Jobs that gets him past his perceptions (based on his own brainstyle) of Jobs' "darker side," which the author feels "bullied" by, to focus on his real strength: envisioning the future, solving problems others have not identified as yet. Jobs does not depend on input from others. Relating to Jobs — *or anyone* — can be disconcerting at best if what you expect is to feel *comfortable.*

On the other hand, the **Conciliator** and the **Deliberator** *depend* on the environment for input, data or readings of others' responses and feelings. They appear interested in others *because of their need for input.* They attend to others — helping or responding. They attend to rules, to information. In fact, these brainstyles seem to look *outside* to define themselves. Internal processing occurs, but does not take the same place in reaching conclusions that it does for the **Conceptor** and **Knower.** Collecting more input is central to the **Conciliator** and **Deliberator.** They can appear as good students. Judged on behaviors alone, they are often described as "victims" who naturally look to others for the answers since, in their perception, "that's where the problem came from in the first place." These are the people who are disturbed by the cranky team member, the social injustice, the rule breakers. They are the compassionate social changers who want to feel more comfortable in the world they inhabit by establishing their own rules to make that world right. In other words, *they want to organize the way they get input.*

Watching how people talk and act without regard to brainstyle or the underlying gifts (visible at **Time Zero**) will also get you into organizing the world to get the input the way you want it. This will never produce satisfaction. Our senses demand that we measure others against our own brainstyle, that what we think is *right* is measured the same way. The judgments that follow are certain to continue separating people rather than empowering relationships. Honoring the differences between each of the four brainstyles will mean taking into account that *this is just their way — it isn't personal* — and designing solutions to educate and influence one another to take into consideration how others take in information. This awareness is what must be learned.

Retrieving What is Filed: The Process is the Same

At **Time Zero** the **Deliberator** stores "as is": unaltered information, specific examples, details. **Deliberators** most often have "terrific memories."

The **Knower** quickly sorts new information, makes a decision based on logic, and files a conclusion. Conclusions go in and conclusions or whole chunks of information come back out almost exactly as they went in.

At **Time Zero** the **Conciliator** attaches information to emotions and stores both together. The **Conciliator** *makes sense* of things by connecting with previous experience or with feeling-based conclusions previously stored. These seem to be accessed or remembered with a random or imaginative, often visual sensory, process. Conversations are often on many topics at once, one subject sparking another. When talking to a more left-brain, or structured person, one or the other can get very irritated at the process. The right brain does not structure or organize according to what is linear; it organizes on an intuitive rationale of its own. Recollections are made frequently when images, sounds, smells, or feelings re-ignite them. The spontaneous response of the right brain is to freely associate ideas and responses. Thus, even factual information recalled by the **Conciliator** has associations connected to it.

A business team in Denver had an issue similar to that of a business team in Pittsburgh. Led by **Conciliators,** both teams were conducting their meetings similarly: holding lengthy sessions with an array of opinions on every subject. The meetings were not balanced with structure, logic and decisiveness. Both teams were made up of **Conciliators** and **Deliberators.** To focus their strengths, we recommended a meeting structure to clarify decisions to be made. This demanded preparation, and limited the discussion to some items that were critical, or moved the discussion outside the meeting altogether. The need for discussing the feelings and meanings of each issue will not be denied to **Conciliators;** but it can be focused to the team's or individual's advantage.

The **Conceptor** takes in both literal and imaginative information in summary form at **Time Zero.** He files holistic *concepts* (thought forms that include randomly accessed, left- and right-brain images, sensory information, and data). Needing little external information, the **Conceptor** spends a lot of time in a random access mode, making associations with a wide range of ideas. He examines what is and *isn't* there and proposes generalizations on the topic. Concepts are posed as trial conclusions that are both factual and emotional. The difference between the random access of the right-brained **Conciliator** and the holistic approach of the left brain/right brain **Conceptor** is that logic and fact play a much greater part in the thinking process for the **Conceptor.**

Making Decisions

At <u>**Time Zero,**</u> when new information is presented, people react by retrieving information in the manner in which their brain dictates they perceive and process it. It is at this critical juncture that the brainstyle is exhibited unaltered and we can identify it.

No matter what your brainstyle, a decision is articulated in the left brain just before it is put into action. For that decision to be a commitment — a decision that is followed through over time — it is necessarily reached by a process that involves both the left and right sides of the brain. A decision does not necessarily occur when someone says, "I've made a decision."

For example, in a meeting where all four brainstyles are present, each of the four will approach a decision at a different speed and with a different perception.

For the **Knower**, a minimal *initial* interchange of new information will occur between both sides of the brain. The logical left brain dominates. It files, concludes, decides, and takes action (all left-brain functions). The **Knower** will quickly conclude about a topic on the basis of his or her own selection of facts, logic and how that logic predicts the future. **Emotions** seem to **later support** the decisions made by the left side. By definition, emotions are rarely a large factor in the **Knower's** decisions.

For the **Conciliator,** the first response (at <u>**Time Zero**</u>) seems to be an intuitive, feeling-based reaction, which later is influenced by facts, other alternatives, or opinions processed in the left side. That is why the **initial "decision" is more a report of a reaction than a decision,** or a real commitment that will be followed through. The **Conciliator** can react quickly with a "gut response" based on intuition, and a spontaneous reaction to the situation. He or she, at the moment, may imagine a positive or negative future for the project. The initial decision is most apt to change when influenced by other arguments — either rational or emotional — when other possibilities are brought in that temper the original picture foreseen by this imaginative brainstyle.

For the **Deliberator,** a search of memory banks can produce a quick decision only if an earlier and similar situation is already stored there. Otherwise, it seems, the **Deliberator** must **systematically proceed from the known to deal with an unknown situation,** *a step at a time.* This requires a variable amount of time and thought and data. (Time is very relative for *all* brainstyles. There are *rapid* and *delayed* processors, within a brainstyle, as well as between different brainstyles.) A **Deliberator** simply cannot make as rapid a decision about something *new* as the other brainstyles. He will slow down and attempt to structure the decision-making process. Do not confuse this brainstyle with a **Knower** when the fast decisions pour from the expert **Deliberator** who has a lot of experience in an area.

The **Conceptor** retrieves concepts that spawn a whole school of associations, both logical and illogical. Creating a decision for the future is an extension of existing concepts, using the same process of high-speed, left-right-left-right brain interaction. After sorting through the **Time Zero** event for a period of time (again, this is relative — but often it is comparatively a rapid process), the **Conceptor** is ready to roll — with several conclusions that qualify as "overview" and allow for a lot of room to move. The **Conceptor** makes an early "umbrella decision," which is actually a *direction* for future decisions that allow for flexibility of action later. Because of this, **Conceptors** can look vague and elusive at first. They are thinking of what steps are *do-able*, what it will *look like* to realize the results — <u>not</u> what it will take to execute the decision (just how are we going to get there?). They are enraptured with the idea and its future possibilities. The specific decisions will come after the overview is established.

> *BrainStyle Clue:*
>
> *Once you understand how different brainstyles file and retrieve information, you will know how to make requests that suit others' brainstyles and how to influence their decisions, and you will be aware of what kind of promises they can truly make about what they can deliver.*

Where Are You?

You may already have some idea of how you fit — or how you think you *should* fit — in this system of brainstyles. But before you decide absolutely that you must be one and not another, keep these things in mind:

ONE: There are no bad brainstyles, just bad fits. There is no brainstyle that by definition is smarter, stronger, or worthier than any other brainstyle. Each strength has its blessings and its pain. Each *brainstyle* carries with it its good news and bad news, has its share of good guys and bad guys, as well as its bright ones and slow ones. You may not even <u>like</u> other people in your own brainstyle … at first. (This changes with increased self-acceptance.)

By knowing your brainstyle and embracing it and all its gifts, you can explore its depths and develop it to its maximum potential. When you know the strength of your personal brainstyle, you can market it to others and create realistic expectations in the minds of family, teachers, bosses, associates, and employees.

It is hard to see the value of continuing year after year to be upset by unrealistic expectations for what people cannot deliver while not fully valuing the gifts they really can. Yet this is all too often how business, schools, and even families operate.

TWO: You don't have to be good at things you are lousy at. All brainstyles are complementary: each excels in some business functions and not in others. The **Knower** manages systems better than does any other brainstyle, but doesn't do as well at managing people. The **Conceptor** is better at seeing the big picture than at getting the right answers. The **Conciliator** is better with people than with systems; the **Deliberator** is better at improving a system than at creating one.

> **Knowing your *brainstyle* is the beginning of an honest relationship...with yourself.**

THREE: Brainstyles cannot be learned. Your brainstyle is part of your personal package. The term brainstyle describes how your brain generates your unique gifts, your strengths. You cannot learn to be some other brainstyle. You can learn to do specific things that other brainstyles do, but never as well as you perform with your natural strengths. Nor will you gain the satisfaction that comes from using your own brainstyle. What you really can learn is to take your own strengths and make them brilliant by using them well.

FOUR: People in the same brainstyle can appear very different. Brainspeed is a relative term. The only scientist (Eysenck) to really study the speed of neural firings has tied this speed to problem-solving abilities. We suspect that there is a great variation in speed of processing within a brainstyle that will look slower or faster in behavior. Colleagues in the same brainstyle can look or sound very different and have different values and preferences. Certainly learned behavior makes people look very different and that is what we always focus on. Look underneath *what* is being talked about for *how* the person is talking about it. Then you will find what you really have in common.

Okay, so you **can't change your brainstyle. You <u>can</u> change how you market your strengths, and this can change your relationships.** You can't really change your brainstyle any more than you can really change the color of your eyes. When you are clear about your strengths, you can show others where you *fit*, so their expectations are realistic. What you <u>can</u> change is how you believe in and sell yourself.

As soon as people hear "you can't change" they get afraid. The fear is "I'm stuck with another label that will limit my future." But consider this: **Brainstyles don't <u>make</u> boxes — they eliminate the discomfort of having them.**

Your brainstyle is your territory, and knowing it lets you claim it. By understanding your *limits*, you can begin a growth process that is *limitless*. Your territory is vast. In fact, you may never discover how expansive it is — you will only know that you are comfortable there. People who have learned this system feel an enormous sense of relief from vainly trying to lay claim to others' territories (sets of strengths) where they feel pushed, misunderstood, and overwhelmed by "shoulds" ("You should be more organized" "You should learn to be more comfortable with people").

Currently almost every boss demands that his employees fit into his or her expectations. Expectations based on what makes him *comfortable* is a box for <u>you</u>. Teaching your boss what you can really deliver can open doors for both of you.

The way to maximize people's capabilities is to understand and accept what they truly are. By exploring brainstyles, you can unleash the formidable power of your individual potential to manage yourself, your relationships, and your career. When that potential is applied to business, the results will be explosive.

BrainStyles Operate The Same Way In Men and Women

Sex differences have been dwelt upon for centuries. Brainstyles makes it apparent that how the brain functions to process information is primarily the same in men and women; it is the *learned behavior* that is different. In our experience, both men and women who process information as a **Conciliator** — with a rapid right-brain response — identify themselves as "feeling, people-people."[4] The men often demonstrate less emotion on an issue-by-issue basis because, they say, they have learned over the years to "control [their] reactions." In a controversial new book, *Brain Sex: The Real Difference Between Men and Women* (Lyle Stuart, 1991), British geneticist Anne Moir asserts that hormones affect men's and women's brains so that they "process information in a different way, which results in different perceptions, priorities and behaviors." When comparing men and women of the same brainstyle, those differences are greatly reduced if not insignificant. Surveying many experts, the article reports "(V)irtually all scientists emphasize they are talking about averages, and there is much overlap between the sexes."[5]

It is entirely possible that there is a higher incidence of one sex in a given brainstyle. Some of the initial research on brain and gender indicates this may be so. But it is not true for *everyone.* Brainstyles works for *both* men and women with the same strengths.

Research in the 1980's on how the brain is organized was reported in several articles by Dr. Doreen Kimura.[6] Her findings show that there are some physiological differences between men and women for very specific abilities (producing speech, making hand movements, defining words) but not for others:

> Kimura is finding in preliminary studies that men tend to be larger on the right side, women larger on the left. These somatic [body] sizes, which may be reflected in differences in the brain hemispheres, correspond to performance on certain tests. 'Things like math are better in right larger individuals, and the trends are the same in males and females', Kimura says.[7] [emphasis added]

More recent research by Roger Gorski, Ph.D., a neuroendocrinologist at the UCLA School of Medicine[8] reports hardwiring differences between the sexes including: a larger corpus callosum in women, more specialization, on average, of speech in the left hemisphere of men, and 15% larger brain mass in men than women. Only one major difference has been observed *in general:* men are better in tests of spatial reasoning and women are better linguistically. Exceptions jump to mind: the female architect and the articulate male writer. The important thing just may be the recognition of brain-based differences that increases our appreciation of who we are *biologically*.

Overall, Moir joins another author, Joe Tanenbaum, author of *Male and Female Realities: Understanding The Opposite Sex*[9] in concluding that men and women are different *as an entire gender*. The differences we are focusing on in our social lives, as in the book *You Just Don't Understand*[10] in which men are classified as "literal" speakers and women as more intuitive, has to mean that all men are rapid left-brain thinkers and women are rapid right-brain. Perhaps the culture demands this, but our brains do not. There will be noticeable similarities in the way same-brainstyle people process information whether man or woman. Women **Knowers** have the same communication issues that men **Knowers** do, with the added complication that most people *expect* women to think and act more like a **Conciliator** or a **Deliberator.** Moir and Tanenbaum add to the expectation that we all act alike based on sex.

Our current data base of over 600 individuals, primarily from business settings, shows the following distribution of brainstyles:

Deliberators,	48.4%	**Conciliators,**	34.3%
Knowers,	11.1%	**Conceptors,**	6.2%

Within the total sample, the distribution of brainstyles by gender is:

Total Male Population: 379   Total Female Population: 233

Male **Deliberators**	50.9%	Female **Deliberators**	44.2%
Male **Conciliators**	28.0%	Female **Conciliators**	44.6%
Male **Knowers**	13.0%	Female **Knowers**	8.2%
Male **Conceptors**	8.1%	Female **Conceptors**	3.0%

All brainstyles have male and female representatives. As you can see, male **Deliberators** are the greatest percentage of the population. Of the female population there seems to be a smaller number of **Conceptor** and **Knower** women. One neurophysiologist's

studies show "women's brains have more gray matter than men's —
nerve tissue that facilitates organizing and processing information
locally in the brain." He concludes that this means women's brains
"could favor any work requiring depth in one specific area."[11] Is this
because his sample was made up of the **Deliberator** brainstyle? Or
would it be likely that more **Conciliators** were examined in Moir's
brain study so that she declares that "Women will see a problem
from all angles, they will read faces, body language" that men won't
see? Moir and others conclude from those studied that women have
a larger *corpus callosum* (connection between the right and left
hemispheres) and therefore have more intuition than men. Men,
she predicts are more linear.[12] Our sample indicates that many, but
certainly not a majority of each sex fits this conclusion.

We say that men and women in the same brainstyle exhibit the
same strengths at **Time Zero.** Research can be helpful if we can use
it to include everyone. Societal ideals — cultural models — (for
how you "should" behave) have made it "right" and "wrong" to be
who you are. It is the judgments about what we've learned that
don't work, that create barriers between people. Let's simplify: the
brain defines the way we think and approach problems. **Women
and men approach decisions by brainstyle** — the speed of the
interaction between right and left hemisphere brain-functions, *no
matter where they are located in the brain complex itself.* Not all
women process information the same way. Nor do all men.

Decisions (which include values and ethics) and information
processing (which includes aptitudes and knowledge) are what
companies — and even spouses — count on. The differences
addressed by *gender* are *not* the critical factors in assessing
strengths. Vive la difference — but look beneath the surface.

Now let's get the job done. Together.

Note: The gender examples in the text will be based on the idea
      that both men and women are valid examples. *He* and *she* are
      used based on this understanding.

PART II: THE FOUR BRAINSTYLES

Before you proceed any further, you may wish to determine your own brainstyle. If so, please turn to Appendix B: *The BrainStyle Inventory.* Then the descriptions in the next four chapters will have more personal meaning.

Chapter Three

The Knower

CHAPTER THREE

THE KNOWER

to know: to perceive or understand clearly and with certainty; to have fixed in the mind or memory

At **Time Zero** the **Knower** initiates a linear, definitive response from the left brain. This left-brain response structures, evaluates, and focuses on a bottom-line result with rapid-fire precision. After some time has elapsed, the right brain alters that pure left-brain response with feeling or emotion. But it doesn't alter it much. To illustrate the rapid surge from left to right and the delayed response from the right-brain functions, the following image uses arrows. In reality, the communications go back and forth underneath the part of the brain that is pictured, through a series of "cables" or networks called the *corpus callosum.*

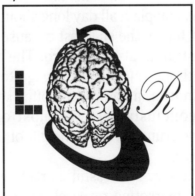

At **Time Zero** the **Knower** doesn't spend much time with people explaining why, or dealing with reasons or needs. The **Knower** delivers an answer.

This is the **Knower's** *brainstyle strength.* He, or she, gets things moving. When properly deployed, the streamlined elegance of a linear, logical response to a new situation affords almost instant clarity and direction. This is vital to any company. The **Knower** can take complexities, simplify them, and nail them down to something do-able.

According to the data we have collected on over 600 business people, **Knowers** are a small minority of the business community. Our research shows they are about 11% of the population, with female **Knowers** about one-third of the group. There is a lack of understanding and sympathy for this brainstyle very often. This may be true partly because they are so few in number.

Decision Making

Confronted with a new and unanticipated situation, the **Knower** has a formidable advantage in being quick, decisive, and to the point. Language comes to us from the left side of the brain and so does sequential logic. When you can combine logic and language without having to take feelings into account, as is the case with the **Knower** at **Time Zero**, the delivery has a certain punch. In verbal battles, **Knowers** tend to "win."

Think about it. When do you hesitate to voice an opinion? When you think you might hurt someone else's feelings? Create conflict? Be wrong? You can complain all day long about a **Knower's** decision and it won't affect him in the slightest because he is unencumbered by right-brain restraints at **Time Zero.** The response comes out automatically without emotional baggage to slow it down. This facility puts the **Knower** in control and often keeps him there — the first and most conclusive answer most often rules the day, especially in a time-crunch. This is the gift of the left brain: to sort, to judge, to organize.

Jan has been a very successful marketing executive for many years, heading up marketing research in major corporations and advertising agencies, and currently is a consultant. What does she bring? "In market research you get overwhelmed with data. I can boil it down and make it simple very quickly. Clients love it. To cut to the main idea and put it in useable terms has focused the account — several times." She is also a very inventive brainstormer. Her job is to participate with both the "creative types" and the "analytical types" to come up with new marketing strategies. As she describes this process, she says, "I have no '**Time Zeros**' — I have new problems which I can instantly submit to a process of making analogies: 'What is this like? not like?' — then I can move toward some pretty far out conclusions rather quickly." Her awareness of how she operates so efficiently in such an ambiguous situation is a hallmark of the focused left brain, applying and directing the mushy stuff that the right brain randomly throws out. She does it with more focus on the future and more clarity than other, more right-brainstyles.

Reactions to this brainstyle for those with different <u>brainstyle timing</u> can be to feel "one down," "slow," or just plain inept around all that decisiveness. This is the pitfall of looking only at <u>superficial</u> behavior and not at the underlying brainstyle. Using *The BrainStyles System*™ you learn to value the timing of your <u>own</u> brainstyle as much as any other.

A **Conciliator** met a **Knower** at a party, and after chatting for a while, reported she shared a very tricky family situation that she was trying to unravel with the very articulate and decisive **Knower**. "There were so many *issues* and *feelings* involved — I just couldn't decide what to do. So I asked his advice. He asked me very *penetrating* questions. In five minutes he told me there were only two options, 'one of which was to end the relationship and never look back.' I realized instantly that all my feelings prevented me from considering this choice and that was why the situation got so complex. After considering the idea, she then said she felt "stupid" because "he made it <u>so</u> simple, and came up with it so fast, I was embarrassed that I even <u>had</u> the problem and especially that I'd shared it with <u>him</u>." Luckily she mentioned this in an indirect way and he was able to explain how easy it was to "solve someone else's problem." The **Conciliator** had the problem we all have, judging *faster* as *better* — and therefore herself as less able. Using brainstyles means eliminating the comparisons you make *between* brainstyles (different gifts) in order to appreciate the value you *and* the other bring to the problem. When you can give up your position — not your self worth — you can make any relationship work.

For the **Knower,** results appear <u>before</u> the process or the people involved. The **Knower's** formula for doing business is simple: See the goal. Make a plan. Remove the barriers. Execute.

The **Knower** can be decisive, take action, take control, and drive toward a clearly defined goal faster than any other brainstyle. Why? Because reaching a goal requires a series of decisions and at each juncture the **Knower** reacts decisively. The clarity and speed of the left-brain computer at each **Time Zero** along the way processes mainly facts and data, undisturbed by feelings and imaginative detours. This brainstyle gets where it sets out to go. The key is that the **Time Zero** response is the *definitive* one for the **Knower** — more so than for any other brainstyle.

> When I know the goal, I can see all the things that have to be done to get there clearer than anyone. With people, I have to make a real determined effort to listen. I get very busy anticipating my answer as well as what they're going to say. 'What's on my mind is on my tongue.' This was especially true when I was younger.[1]

Because we prize comfort in our relationships instead of contribution, we label the **Knower's** strength *inflexibility* and dismiss it rather than exploring how to make the best use of this strength.

Case in point: Steve, a **Knower,** is a manager in a major insurance firm. One of his sales people is a high-potential person, someone Steve has identified as having unlimited promise. The problem is that the man cannot handle his personal finances. He is so far in debt that the pressure of creditors is beginning to interfere with his work. He faces personal bankruptcy.

Without making things personal in any way, Steve immediately sets up a plan of action to *eliminate* the problem. See the goal. Make a plan. Do it. Period. He has his wife (a financially skillful **Deliberator**) take over managing his salesperson's personal finances. He removes the impediment to work. He does not take this action because he feels sorry for the man or because stepping in and taking over is a kind thing to do. Those would be right-brain responses. Taking over "just makes sense" to Steve.

(Incidentally, it is unlikely that any of the other brainstyles would have presumed to take charge of another person's personal affairs in the name of logic. But the fact is that Steve achieved his immediate goal — to have a productive employee — in the most direct way possible.)

BrainStyle Clue:

Knowers *get into trouble expecting others to make decisions as quickly as they do. Still, don't ask a* **Knower** *to "be patient." Influence him early. Spend time on the bottom-line result (goal) you're after. Tell it; sell it. It must be logical. Once the decision is made, it's made.*

Conflict

Knowers, by definition, are absolutely clear on their goals: they want control; they want results. They appear inflexible. They often are, but only because they have personally worked through the problem so logically that to them there is no other plausible way to achieve the goal in question. The appropriate steps seem obvious, even necessary. A logical plan backed up by hard facts is <u>worth</u> defending. And so, once they have committed to an idea, they will use their powerful logic to argue their view. Such a defense is not "confrontation" to the **Knower.** A critical point to know about this brainstyle group is that they respect people who respond directly. The eyeball to eyeball presentation of your case is what they desire and you don't have to think like a **Knower** to do this. Just be direct with information. Often, they will stop and listen. They will attend to an approach that is as straight from the shoulder as is their own. The **Knower** calls it being <u>direct</u>; at least two other brainstyles call it "steamrolling." The only problem is the *interpretation* ("steamrolling") attached to the behavior by a different brainstyle.

One of the authors sat next to a division president of a major airline on a recent flight from Seattle to Dallas. After a short conversation, it was apparent he was a **Knower.** He described meetings with his boss in which exchanges were heated. In one such meeting a wristwatch was thrown against the wall. "Everyone else was either looking at their shoes or got up and left. I didn't mind. I just looked up and said, 'Good, is it time to start the meeting now?'" There was nothing scary in the outburst or the confrontation to the **Knower.** He had already decided the wrist watch thrower was not serious. When this brainstyle has decided something, they are gifted at not allowing emotions to influence them.

The real issue? <u>**Time.**</u> Just because different brainstyles function at different speeds does not mean that one is better than another. The rapid left-brain response means facts up front. Most often the **Deliberators** and **Conciliators** are uncomfortable with this speed, and so call the **Knower** a bully. If other brainstyles would not compete with this strength, but rather use their own strengths and timing to respond and build on what is offered, enormous gains in productivity could be made. The <u>worst</u> thing to do is to judge **Knower** behavior as "overbearing" or a **Knower** response as "intimidating." Such pre-judgments are the cause of "poor communications" and will impede your capacity to hear what is really meant. You can take it personally and lose the point and probably the relationship. The only way the **Conciliator** and many **Deliberators** can work with this brainstyle is to focus on the content and forget the delivery.

BrainStyle Clue:

Knowers *rarely get into "conflicts" or "attack" others. These are the perceptions of <u>other</u> brainstyles.* **Knowers** *are <u>direct</u>. They use left-brained language which measures and evaluates. To discuss an emotional subject with a* **Knower,** *rehearse it so it is not so personal for you.*

The **Knower** comes to the table with logic, judgments, and facts so tightly packed around an argument that there seems to be no soft spot left for negotiation. Through reading or interviewing others, she builds arsenals of facts selected to make the best argument possible — a winner. Often for the **Knower** it is only win or lose, right or wrong — because the left brain operates this way. Indeed, the brainstyles-illiterate Knower may even evaluate right-brain activities, such as consensus and compromise, as losing.

BrainStyle Clue:

*The ways in which interactions with a **Knower** get to be win or lose situations relate directly to brain speeds at **Time Zero:***

- **The Conciliator** responds emotionally at **Time Zero.** In business, logic "wins" or at least overpowers.

Conciliators: prepare for emotional subjects. Ask for a "time-out."

- **The Deliberator** asks questions at **Time Zero.** The **Knower** decides.

Deliberators: get data ahead. Consider the **Knower** a decision-making ally.

- **The Conceptor** gets conceptual and can't return detail as quickly, shot-for-shot, at **Time Zero.**

Conceptors: discuss the long-term goals with a **Knower**; let the **Knower** handle the details. Be direct about problems.

- Other **Knowers?** You can fight to the death if you choose to, or you can find common ground from which to launch a project.

By not recognizing that "being right" so fast means literally *interfering* with the timing of other brainstyles at **Time Zero,** the **Knower** misses opportunities to influence effectively. Other brainstyles need time to process, react, or listen. This most basic interaction is defined by brainstyle, not "intelligence."

> *BrainStyle Clue:*
>
> *There is only one turf on which to engage in battle with a **Knower:** the goals. As long as you try to fight on details, you can't win. The **Knower** will get locked in. Change the arena and move the discussion to the Big Picture or desired result.*

A **Knower** can (quickly) **tell** an employee what to do, but will that person really do it? Using natural strengths, the **Knower** can spend time in the **Knower's** version of *coaching* about what the goal is and how to reach it, systematically. Allowing time for others to change means patience is required for this part of the job, and it is often in short supply for the **Knower** brainstyle. Moreover, people with other brainstyles will have different approaches to getting the job done as well as different ways they like being *coached.* **Knowers** are not empathizers. Conflict can start when time and <u>brainstyle</u> <u>timing</u> are not taken into account. The **Knower** needs to remind herself that <u>quick</u> <u>does</u> <u>not</u> <u>equal</u> <u>competent</u>. As they say, you can always tell a **Knower,** but you can't tell her much.

Case in Point: A good example of a **Knower** using his strengths came from a salesman, Lenny. A customer was describing his relationship with Lenny: "I got so mad at him, it wasn't funny. I told him his product was the worst I'd ever used, he was the most obnoxious sales guy I'd ever dealt with, and when that didn't faze him, I threw him out. But Lenny kept coming back. My tirades didn't seem to bother him. It was incredible. He never moved off the goal. He took all the abuse I could muster and never reacted. No other salesman would have — *could* have stood it. He just kept coming back and telling me how he was fixing our problems. And darned if I didn't give him back the business."

The lack of feeling in an emotional situation was Lenny's strength. His structure of the situation was to solve the problems and get to the goal. He "won" (as a **Knower** would say).

Management Potential

The **Knower** may quickly reach the top management team. Why? Because he is able to make his views sound inevitable in the left-brained, measurable world of business. The **Knower** can be indispensable. He is a forceful negotiator who uses a solid line of logical details to defend his vision and its monetary value. As long as doing business equals getting results, the smart **Knower** can climb swiftly up the promotion ladder.

Vision and creativity for this brainstyle can be defined very differently than for those with other brainstyles. It should be apparent by now that the leap into the future for the **Knower** will be a more practical move than for most of the rest of the group. By collecting disjointed facts or examples, the hard-charging **Knower** can convert a synthesis of information into a fairly rapid number of future possibilities. The thing that characterizes the **Knower's** vision and distinguishes it from the **Conceptor,** for instance, is that there is a consistent *practical* theme to the future solutions. Right or wrong, the vision is one which applies existing technology or current ideas in ways that *make sense,* apply what is known for *use* by someone. They are new, and they are usually specific. Brainstorming for a **Knower** will be ingenious new ways to look at old news — an invaluable resource for any enterprise that wants to move forward. In contrast, the visionary **Conceptor** may reach a final solution that is as workable, but the process of getting to it will not be nearly as clear or rational along the way.

Bo, a high-energy, well-disciplined **Knower,** was spotted while still in his twenties as a young man who could turn around a company, deliver more business ideas and results faster than anyone else in the European trading conglomerate in which he worked. In conferences with his boss, the CEO, he would propose lists of new ways to manage the multi-billion dollar U.S. holdings for the firm. As he moved on to become a private entrepreneur, Bo used the same tireless process of developing contacts, reading and collecting diverse information and sorting it into new business opportunities. One small venture of many was begun when he heard of the new regulations for and access to 800 numbers for businesses. He currently owned a music business that sold tapes of prerecorded music to radio stations. After many conversations with many more people, a brainstorming session with his **Conciliator** wife (a supportive good listener), he came up with a new, yet focused solution: a 900 number (pay-per-call) request line for "Hot Hits". The solution applied existing resources and made new uses of new technology in several new ways.

Management systems (as in Management by Objectives) that value and reward *results first* promote this brainstyle. Unfortunately this gives the **Knower** no real preparation for management, which requires skill in the **Knower's** *non-strength:* dealing with people and their irrational, non-linear emotions.

Knowers who include people in the plan have a better chance of having plans implemented. They will not naturally do so. "Relationships take tremendous effort," as Bo put it. And when your efforts are naturally focusing on the task at hand, you do not have the time to be a friend. Relationships have a purpose — just because everything has a purpose for a **Knower.** They do not have the need for a friend just to have a friend. They do not deal with people by "empathizing" or "understanding" in the way that other brainstyles do. As one **Knower** recalled, "I've learned to call in the 'sweepers' — they clean up after I've put my foot in my mouth. They listen and talk nice and I keep my mouth shut." This **Knower** knew he couldn't pretend to do something he wasn't good at.

Knowers help others see where they want to go. They challenge plans — in words others say can come across "like a hammer." Hurt feelings can result for those who focus on the words. **Knowers** help get past the right brain — into focus with the facts, with organization, and with words to make it happen. They demand *action* in service of a *goal*. "I'm willing to be screamed at and not be afraid," says the turnaround specialist who first fires former employees before restaffing in the new image.

The **Knower** gives unquestioned loyalty and support to his subordinates *after making an initial decision that they are on his team.* Then he must leave them to do their best, ask for results, and hold their feet to the fire on meeting targets. "Once you get through the bark, the guy's a 'softie'" is the kind of comment made about **Knowers** on many occasions. In fact, **Knowers** see themselves as tender-hearted and most often misunderstood as "tough," when in fact all they are trying to do is bring logic to a messy situation without all the extra emotion of the **Conciliator** or the extra steps of the **Deliberator.**

When the **Knower** supports *your* goals, he is a powerful ally. If he has another agenda, watch out. He will go to the mat for a goal of his own. This brainstyle is a focused, conclusive one.

Often, the **Knower** makes a better consultant or expert (non-manager) than manager. Dealing with people by providing direction is most natural; this brainstyle is best equipped to provide inputs that are logical and lend themselves to the laws of thermodynamics. **Knowers** who must manage people can team up with a brainstyle that handles people issues naturally and can influence the **Knower** on *how* projects get done. Or, addressing the topic logically, a **Knower** can learn some systematic ways to collect input from others more often. Listening, as others want to be listened to, is a non-strength for the **Knower.** If you're this brainstyle, you need to tell others to expect to be listened to for content and focus.

The **Knower** makes the ideal turn-around officer. He is the one who can come into a troubled company, review the plan, separate the wheat, fire the chaff, and come out with a fresh loaf. Then he may need to move on to another "field," where gifts for swift decisions will be appreciated. Because once the chaos is stabilized with logic and a firm hand, the equilibrium will require different strengths. Putting another brainstyle in the second spot with control of the daily management is not a bad solution when the **Knower** cannot move on.

Case in point: Take the Frank Lorenzo story, as reported in

Fortune's cover article "America's Toughest Bosses."[2] Here was the ideal person for coming in as CEO and pulling off a turn-around for the troubled Continental and Eastern Airlines. But problems surfaced in his area of *non-strength* — people — unionized people, at that — as he tried moving the old culture of *beliefs* and *values* (right-brain notions) to a more hard-line, measurable, fiscally viable one. Others could not join him in this kind of change and in the time frame that Lorenzo (his **Knower** brainstyle) could work in. His Waterloo was not being able to get enough people to enroll in his vision of the future. Fast and early decisions established an inner circle *vs.* enemies. The company became a battle-ground where you either won or lost. As the head of Texas Air, he did it his way or no way at all, and was willing to go out fighting.

Control and expediency do not produce loyalty or, it seems, change. Lorenzo's tremendous commitment to a new order did not create a similar commitment in his followers.

> Frank Lorenzo of Texas Air might be called many things. He is a visionary, a dealmaker, a union buster, and showboater. But to Lorenzo's subordinates, "loose cannon" probably fits him best. For Lorenzo, 48, sometimes creates as much havoc among his crew as he creates among the competition.
>
> Two chains of command lead to the top of Texas Air. One is the official hierarchy of line managers. The other is a small cadre of executives with whom Lorenzo feels personally at ease and whom he uses for special projects and to gather information. [This cadre is his] junta of 'bright young entrepreneurs to challenge the system.'
>
> Lorenzo uses this cadre to perform staff functions. Often he ends up undermining his line managers. According to several former employees, Lorenzo assigns lower-echelon people to projects that their bosses are unaware of. Or he recommends

to members of his fifth column that they not support their superiors' plans. Says a former executive: 'Planning is impossible.' Observes another: 'You never know who's on your team, so you are always off balance. The intrigue is incredible.'[3]

Lorenzo, certainly a **Knower,** with an eye on the balance sheet and clearly defined goals, was operating for the economic survival of the company. He used a "fifth column" as the most expedient way to get results. But the existing culture saw only that he operated without "care" for their political (personal) agendas and established hierarchy. They didn't get included in setting policies or goals. The more his position was challenged, the more intractable he became. Strikes didn't work. Chaos in the minds of others seemed to leave him unperturbed. His gift was to bring clarity and so, by definition, it was a "lonely" job. Lorenzo had a vision, and the fact that he could not get other people to see it as he did was undoubtedly as baffling as it was personally painful to him. He did not have a way to build a consensus. He did not understand the timing of how other brainstyles process information. He also did not appreciate other brainstyles' need for more information (explanations, background, etc.) in order to proceed. Small issues, but critical to moving an organization.

Delegation

The **Knower** sees what needs to be done but has a hard time getting people to do it. The gift of the pure left-brain response is that she who possesses it can cut to the core and figure out what needs to be *done* faster than anybody else. But that does not thereby make her a consensus builder. Basically, the **Knower** doesn't naturally trust people who are slower to understand what (in the **Knower's** perception) the job involves. As the **Knower** might judge, the **Conciliator** is wishy-washy, the **Deliberator** slow and indecisive, the **Conceptor** off the wall. Another **Knower** is, as often as not, just wrong.

The danger lies in the **Knower's** trying to sell the whole package at **<u>Time Zero.</u>** Other brainstyles cannot assimilate it then. *People interactions require timing and that timing must be based on their brainstyles.*

Because **Knowers,** like all other brainstyles, give trust to those they are comfortable with and because they are comfortable only with a fraction of those with their own brainstyle, they do not trust many people, hence do not delegate well. Moreover, the act of delegation, which requires both trust and release of control, is doubly classified as a *non-strength* — albeit a skill basic to managing people and running a company. True, a **Knower** will take charge faster than any other brainstyle (remember General Alexander Haig's famous statement: "I'm in charge here" that came *too* quickly after President Reagan's attempted assassination?) He structures. He orders. He tells you what to do. But <u>telling</u> is not the same thing as delegating.

The Knower does not naturally delegate well. Why? Delegation involves giving another person both authority and responsibility. It means giving someone else *control.* Delegating starts with the words "You be in charge of..." It shouldn't be confused with an assignment, which includes no authority and possibly only a little responsibility. An assignment starts with the words "You do ..."

For the young **Knower,** limited skill at delegating creates few problems. Traveling fast and alone means traveling light. But as she is promoted, there is more to attend to than the systems she has devised and the goals she's after. Typically, the high-ranking **Knower** can assign the work on a project to others, with assessments along the way, until the time of the final reckoning. The question is whether the **Knower** ever releases control. Developing others' strengths is the **Knower's** weak suit. As a result, others in the organization fulfill the **Knower's** prophecy: they really <u>can't</u> do it as well.

Case in point: At the end of his career, the single-minded Harold Geneen of ITT left behind him a mixture of powerful feelings: admiration, devotion, fear, and hatred. He built one of the most successful and profitable companies in the shortest period of time on record. He was an extraordinary man. He also left a vacuum created by his hands-on operation of the company.

His strategy for growth was a logical, **Knower** approach: acquire. You don't have to go through the long building process with an acquisition. You find it, buy it, organize it, and run it — more efficiently than the previous owner. And in true **Knower** fashion, Geneen had better systems than anyone else, systems that only he could run. In practice he did not delegate responsibility for growing the acquisitions **he** made. He assumed that responsibility himself, extracting the facts from subordinates in marathon sessions lasting many hours. Feelings were not a concern. Results were paramount. If you were willing to set personal priorities aside, you learned how to operate by the numbers. To him, delegation meant a loss of control — numbers did not — and given the numbers indicating incredible growth, who could question the quality of that control?

ITT's fortunes post-Geneen were an altogether different story. No successor had been developed. No one could run the Geneen system of getting at the "unshakable [financial] facts" with the trial by fire (confrontation and questioning) that were his trademark. No one had the touch. And the bottom line has reflected that ever since. The days of ITT's phenomenal success ended with Geneen.

So what can the **Knower** brainstyle learn from Geneen's as well as Frank Lorenzo's example? *Strengths must be used in service of a larger goal.* The mission or vision of a company must be defined and be defined broadly enough to apply all the strengths of all the players to reach it. When the survival of the company is at stake, as was the case for Eastern Airlines, the main job of the leader is to establish a *context* for all to apply their strengths full out, which means being able to appreciate and use the strengths of the leader as well. Tyranny or top down administrations are irrelevant when it is clear what the overriding priority is. And a **Knower** is more than capable of making this clear. This subject will be explored in Chapter 8: *Where You Can Take Your Brainstyle.*

Case in point: Mike, a **Knower,** is a plant manager in Cranston, Rhode Island. He has been assigned one of the oldest plants in the system, with responsibility to meet an aggressive financial plan. His company has demanded a focus on "people systems." Mike has taken charge with eyes on the goals and made a good plant better, initiating a pilot program relying on employee involvement. He describes his strengths in managing as:

> I believe in being *practical,* getting people motivated by getting excited about the job and then making it believable and do-able. *I take ideas into action.* I set the example by being upfront, direct, with no hidden motives. I build trust with good follow-up.

Mike has initiated some very "conceptual" changes using the strengths of his brainstyle: action, results, a clear focus. He gets people to commit to the goal, and expects the attitude to follow.

Mike is very aware of the "politics" that impinge on his job. With knowledge of brainstyles, the young **Knower** may not make the same mistakes as Lorenzo — ramrodding political solutions instead of working through them. Much as a **Conciliator** is aware of people dynamics, **Knowers** often speak of *agendas* that people have about certain projects. Mike and other **Knowers** are very concerned about impacting others. As under Frank Lorenzo, there is much discussion of how to get projects through the system. Note how Mike has chosen an agenda that involves teamwork, practically demonstrated by the leadership:

> My team (Mike's peers) and my boss need to be more effective liaisons with the field, and set the example for the organization by working more closely with other functions. We'll never get everything done (that we've said we'll do) any other way.

The subject of influencing people is the same as for the right-brainstyles, but the tactics and approach come from the opposite side of the brain.

Whereas the **Conciliator** prefers to influence through relationships and personal liking (*Can you work with her? She's a good person*) the **Knower** influences by matching up agendas. (*She needs information on ___ so she'll work with you.*) And if that doesn't work, there is always the **Knower** caveat: *Just get it done; you don't have to like her.*

BrainStyle Clue:

A ***Knower*** lives to make ideas real — to see the results — in systems and with people. The drive from the left brain propels the ***Knower*** to clear a path for the shortest distance between start and finish. Ensure that the ***Knower's*** agenda includes a broader vision and the values that demand all contribute as a team.

The **Knower** is a natural leader, but rarely a "popular" one. The brainstyle commands respect, not adoration.

Learning

The **Knower** summarizes great chunks of information with breath-taking efficiency. And this is how he does it.

When a **Knower** sets out to learn something, he does so by sorting data, which he files in memory as conclusions or summaries. Put another way, he files or remembers information in left-brain, logical "chunks," not individual details. And so when the **Knower** remembers (retrieves) the *information, it comes back up the same way:* as conclusions. The information gets stored quickly and comes back in rapid, concise summaries. This ability to learn and remember "conclusively," gives the **Knower** the appearance of being a "quick study." The fact that most of the process goes on privately can create the impression that he is "arrogant."

The **Knower** looks very much like a "closed loop" because of the way this brainstyle processes information. Once the **Knower** has organized the supporting evidence into his (internally consistent) conclusions, there is initially very little that anyone can do to persuade him that another system — much less another conclusion — might be superior or at least just as good. Two other brainstyles have the most difficulty with this: the **Conciliator** and the **Deliberator.** Both of these brainstyles process information by constantly getting new inputs and other opinions. This is why you hear comments like "He just won't *listen*" and "I don't know how to influence her. She has a closed mind." The way people process information determines the way they relate to their environment. The internally "complete" **Knower** does not *need* people the same way other brainstyles do — *for information* (approval, decisions, new data).

The capacity to be persuaded — and be a part of the crowd — depends on right-brain input, and the **Knower** has no ready access to that input.

The young **Knower** characteristically will be the first one to take a stand on an issue — and not care who supports it. More than likely he is interested in technical or practical considerations for his own reasons. **Knowers** are not the social butterflies. They do not care about others' opinions except as those *opinions affect their own achievement.* If the teacher or coach or classmate can get across the idea that how they act or dress will damage or enhance their chances for getting to their goal, they will listen. School can be a place to win for a **Knower** when results are prized. But most often sociability and adaptability are the Citizenship Requirements and lots of negative assessments get made about the **Knower,** who doesn't care about fitting in for the sake of fitting in.

The bookstores are filled with books on how to change the **Knower** who "abuses" the sensibilities of others. Brainstyles that process information differently care greatly about how things are said, and how feelings are considered in the saying. We can get out of the Victim-Persecutor dialogue with respect for **both** brainstyles by keeping the following in mind: The **Knower** is not being "insensitive." In his own left-brain world, he is being direct and factual. So stop taking it personally.

Risk Taking

A Knower doesn't risk, he covers his flank. He improves the odds. He reduces complex situations to formulas, logical strategies. Each brainstyle defines **risk** as "possible loss." The **Knower's** most personal risk is that he or she will be *wrong* — devalued because he is no longer the expert. Winning and losing are part of the game. No problem. But the **Knower** will take precautions not to be proved wrong.

It may sound strange to say that someone who is right out there delivering opinions with expert authority is not a risk-taker — especially of the damn-the-torpedoes-full-speed-ahead school. That takes much more emotion in the regular course of things. The **Knower** is logical. And as with each brainstyle, this is both the good news about risk-taking and the bad news. Look at a recap of **Knower** brainstyle traits:

1. takes in literal, measurable information naturally
2. makes fast decisions by sorting and judging quickly
3. uses information that is encountered later to support initial conclusions
4. stays "in control" (doesn't re-sort the information readily)
5. knows exactly what needs to be done according to plan
6. likes to work and decide alone
7. learns by getting the conclusion first, then adding the facts to support it.
8. works in the future by combining today's ideas in new ways to come to innovative applications for tomorrow.

Here's how the **Knower** brainstyle acts in response to risk:

• He looks to the future and then formulates goals or new synergies of ideas based on things already known. Here the strengths of logic come into play. Dealing with risk means dealing with the unknown. The **Knower** tries to make the future a logical certainty, if not a verifiable one.

• After the initial brainstorming and leap into the future, the ability to assess and structure mean a plan to *prevent things from going wrong.* The left brain does *not* plan *for what can go right.* Compared to **Conceptors** and **Conciliators,** there is little optimism in the **Knower's** system even though there may be a great deal of confidence and positive support for others. The **Knower** would say there is *realism.* There *is* focus and a drive to the goal. *Most Knower's systems are grounded in practicality as well as problem prevention, not possibility thinking.* Success is often defined as "staying ahead of the game." Other brainstyles want the leap into the unknown to have some (emotional) "hope." **Knowers** don't deal comfortably with a vague "dream." They are too practical.

• Risk requires flexibility, the willingness to change as often as change is required. **Knowers** will change <u>tactics</u> on a dime. When better options are available they will take them. But major directions are hard to redefine for this brainstyle. It's easier to stop, cut bait and start over. *Structure* and *change* are contradictions. And structure is the strength of this brainstyle.

• A **Knower** prefers working alone partly because he distrusts the processes others use (slower or less logical = less competent for many **Knowers**). Trust is what allows a leap into the unknown. Trust is what attracts a network of support to deal with mistakes. **Collaboration** is a non-strength of the **Knower.**

• The **Knower** makes fast, logical decisions that eliminate having to deal with emotional input. **Risk is profoundly emotional** for most. If the logical answer doesn't carry the day, **Knowers** cannot influence outcomes.

Case in point: When the opportunity to invest in a new business arose, Sam, a **Knower,** was offered an inside track. But as he studied the deal, challenging it point by point, one conclusion became clear: It was risky. No one could give him a logical scenario for success in the future. There were too many things that could go wrong — even though he would be a central part of the management team who would be influencing the company's outcome. He chose not to invest.

BrainStyle Clue:

*Let the **Knower** tell you what kind of system you'll need to get from here to there. Ask the **Knower** to critique the latest new idea. He'll tell you what can go wrong. When it's time to decide the future, call in the **Knower** when you want "realistic", innovative ideas that will prevent problems and apply solutions in new ways.*

---

*Being the **Knower** can be the most difficult of all.*

The following is an interview with a mature **Knower:**

Q. What are you most proud of?
My biggest contribution was foresight in selecting the company's computer systems. I evaluated one that went against IBM's recommendation. This was a major factor in the successful acquisition of the company. We were running with the lowest data processing costs in the entire new corporation. (**Knower** *contributions: foresight based on fact, taking an unpopular stand, creating efficiencies*)

Q. How have you changed over your career?
When I was younger, I worked everyone eighteen hours a day. I worked all the time. It was all I cared about. In the last ten years, I opened to look at what impact I had on people. I didn't have the words, couldn't see what I was doing. I had heard feedback before, but it just seemed like they were always being defensive. I got new feedback in an atmosphere of trust and support and I took it in — probably for the first time. And I was

over 45. Self-consciousness dropped away and the fear of being rejected. I found out that I overwhelm people with logic. I didn't know I did this. I thought about winning — being right. My self-esteem would suffer if I couldn't win — logically. I was more willing to fight than to be affectionate. I now choose another behavior — not at **Time Zero** — but later. I get my answer quickly. I have started asking the others for theirs too. When I fire out quickly, I clean it up right away. I try to think about it for awhile.

Q. *What are your strengths?*
I am best at goals, systems and controls. I'm most effective in planning and organizing for implementation — to make ideas real. My strength is coaching people in being logical in their approach and solutions. I can question for detail in the steps to implement. The difference between me and a **Deliberator** is *speed and relevance.* They get to the point by going around and around. They use a staff to get all the bits and pieces they can and then synthesize it themselves. There is a lot of overhead. I tend to cut to the chase and limit the problem in the first place. I would be good in a 'turnaround' situation, but I still tend to be authoritarian as a leader.

Corporate Controller, **KNOWER**

As a **Knower,** if that is your case, you recognize that you are often misunderstood. You know your ideas are good, and you know that most of the time you are right about things. You know that you can work a system quicker, faster, more efficiently than anyone else. But sometimes you have trouble persuading other people that your ideas are the best way.

These are your trouble spots: Assessing your total value solely according to the strength of your left-brain speed. Most **Knowers** are locked out of relationships because they come across as "arrogant" — showing that they judge others as less competent. In a results-oriented world, you are faster with an answer. Problem:

You *need more than one* (your) *answer.* And you need commitment to the answer that is reached. Realize that your strength in the left brain means by definition you are not strong in the right brain. And you <u>must</u> use those right-brain strengths of others if you want to create commitment. To deal with people, creativity, and personal motivation, those with other brainstyles will be faster and better at ideas on how to get the whole solution.

Chapter Four

The Conceptor

CHAPTER FOUR

THE CONCEPTOR

kon sept'or:
a person who forms general notions or ideas by mentally combining all the characteristics or particulars

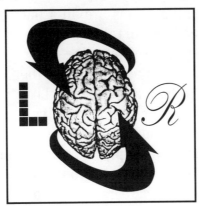

At **Time Zero,** the **Conceptor** delivers a swift, global response processed by both sides of the brain. Information is collected by both right-brain intuition and left-brain judgment. Perception selects from facts and insight. The **Conceptor** is very selective about how much information can be processed at a single time, because it sets off an internal, random search for related concepts that follow a logic personal to the individual and involves a rapid left-right-left-right brain exchange. This exchange leads to rapid conceptual "leaps" about future possibilities which are hard to articulate at first. Many **Deliberators** and **Knowers** find this brainstyle hard to follow. They are "too global," "too general." Their direction-finding can get lost or not appreciated in the flurry of details that follow.

Conceptors, according to the data we have collected, are even scarcer to find than the **Knower** brainstyle. Only about 6% of the sample of over 600 we observed and studied were **Conceptors.** Of this small group, only one-quarter of them were female.

When addressing a complex problem, the holistic approach of

the **Conceptor** can name critical issues, sort priorities and come out with several strategies for getting to the future. The **Conceptor** speaks in a personal "code" (which is how he took in the information — all at once) in which words are charged with many associations and assumptions. **Conceptors** often speak using a deductive process — they know the outcome and don't know why or precisely how they got there — and work backwards to the present. People and systems are all a part of the thinking. The future is the most comfortable playground and creativity in approach and solution is the outcome.

However, just as soon as we say that the **Conceptor** is creative, everybody wants to be that brainstyle. Like "bottom line thinking" and being a "team player," being **creative** has become one of the "shoulds" of the American business culture. The **Conceptor** has the brainstyle best suited to supplying *creativity* and *vision.* That's just how it goes — but it's *not* how *everyone* can go or should go.

In fact, early in their careers **Conceptors** look less like creators than troublemakers. They tend to take rules as starting points instead of stopping points. They can be difficult: "Quiet! I'm doing the talking here! This is MY ...!" (idea, plan, whatever). They insist on creating (using their gift) when all that is needed is replication. Ask a **Conceptor** to build a moveable container, and he is likely to devote valuable resources and time inventing a wheelbarrow that could readily be purchased off the shelf for much less money.

Likewise, creativity without execution is nothing but dreaming, and the *unseasoned* **Conceptor** can be poor at stopping the creative process and settling on an idea to carry through to completion. The **Conceptor's** gift is in supplying the vision and the strategies. Those in other brainstyles are better at evaluating them, attaching costs, and then implementing them.

Case in point: Katie is a **Conceptor** who has learned to focus her strengths and provide direction. An entrepreneur who started and built an interior design firm from scratch in the recession of the early '80's to two offices with some sixty staff by 1989, Katie found a few things she could do better than others and pushed only those.

She says she "tries to discipline her interactions." She has been told that she has a way of focusing <u>all</u> her attention on the client's needs in a project — both personal and professional — to design new solutions that they really appreciate for the fit with their situation. She problem-solves to get maximum creativity for the lowest cost. How? She says she is best as a "hands-off" manager who provides training, overviews, goals — but allows the professionals to "make the details work." She adds, "I'm best at inspiring others — being somewhat clairvoyant, subjective — reading what they're not saying — then putting it into a controlled solution." Katie assesses her strengths with an overview, good in some broad areas like drive, delegation, setting priorities; not good in others — details or execution on a daily basis.

Decision Making

The **Conceptor** makes fairly quick, complete decisions. He may be no match for the **Knower** at the starting gate, but he is quick with a global *response that can set the stage* for making several decisions on the topic. Once the broad direction is stated, or the hypothesis formed, a project can roll out smartly. The **Conceptor's** decision-making process begins with both sides of the brain rapidly supplying input rather than one or the other hemisphere dominating. This is distinctive. But why is it important? Because ultimately, long-term decisions require the best of what the left and right hemispheres of the brain can offer; a complete decision must include the imagination and passion of the right brain and the logic and articulation of the left brain.

People in the **Conceptor** brainstyle often move more quickly to decisions than other brainstyles can reasonably and emotionally follow. At **Time Zero** the **Conceptor** responds with reactions generated by an instantaneous left-brain/right-brain processing. He is general. Sweeping. And often sure — with no proof.

For the sake of comparison, let's look at what happens with all four brainstyles when their **Time Zero** responses encounter outside influences.

• The **Knower** will be influenced least by others' responses. His **<u>Time Zero</u>** response is a definitive one, often a conclusion already formed. A direct challenge to his initial decision is the best way to influence it, before he has had a chance to marshal all facts and feelings in support of it.

• The **Conciliator** is apt to be influenced too much by others' responses. The **<u>Time Zero</u>** right-brain response — either intuitive or emotional — has no words to express itself. In the time needed to pick up some left-brain data or words to support it, the initial idea can easily be replaced by the quick or conclusive statement of another. Spontaneity is often moving around from one exciting idea to another. On the other hand, some **Conciliators** have learned to protect this initial thinking process — by getting defensive or withdrawing — while trying to "sort out their feelings" or the many "pictures" they get during the discussion.

• The **Deliberator** resists influence at **<u>Time Zero</u>** while searching memory and assembling all the information for a decision. Challenges require re-sorting of data. Explanations are preferred that follow a step-by-step thought process. This takes time. Once a decision is made, the **Deliberator** is not very open to changing his mind; he is planning how to reach the goal.

• The **Conceptor** has a *whole brain response in the present moment,* one that can receive and process both facts and especially random insights at **<u>Time Zero</u>** + 1. **Conceptors** cannot attend to (process) great amounts of input. A very few ideas will get their internal processor going. Overviews appear. Monologues erupt to test out ideas. Plans A, B, and C spin from suggestions. Most **Conceptors** demand control during this process. If you are another brainstyle, and you are unused to this process, you may find it very uncomfortable.

The fact that the left/right brain exchange happens so quickly for the **Conceptor** gives this brainstyle a distinct advantage over other brainstyles in the matter of making decisions *that others can enroll in.* Unlike the **Knower,** who quickly makes decisions based strictly on left-brain facts and logic, the **Conceptor** derives decisions from a blend of reason and feelings. The human factor is always a part of the process. Accordingly, soon after **Time Zero,** the **Conceptor** process works best when there are others participating in it — or at least present to hear and appreciate it. In his book interviewing six major business leaders, writer Michael Meyer describes Steven Jobs of Apple Computers, a model **Conceptor:**

> Jobs is at his best in any brainstorming session. A core group of eleven employees is discussing what goals should be, how best to build up the company. Jobs dominates the room. Even when he's not talking, he's moving, exuding energy, guiding the discussion through sheer body language...When he likes something, he gets visibly excited. His eyes light up. He bounces in his seat, paces, gestures. He talks about what NeXT [Jobs' new company] will be like....Jobs shows himself a master at defining priorities, exciting others with his vision of what NeXT can be, clarifying the company's ultimate goals as they move from research through production to the actual marketing of the new computer.[1]

For the **Conceptor**, a decision involves determining what the problem is *and isn't* and then picturing what the future would look like in terms of several solutions to that problem. Of Jobs, Dan'l Lewin says, "Steve is always looking right at the edge of the technological horizon. What can be done now? How do we make the next great leap? Steve's goal in life is to build great products by combining technologies in a way that no one else has."[2]

To get to the future, the **Conceptor** does not have to go into memory stacks the way the **Deliberator** does to see what worked before; and he doesn't attend as closely as the **Conciliator** does to what is available or known on the subject, nor can he do the free-floating, spontaneous brainstorming of the **Conciliator**. The **Conceptor** has a self-contained system that circulates and filters information through feelings and logic. Because memory is accessed as whole "thought balls" of logical and emotional experience, any decision that the **Conceptor** makes is apt to be novel in some significant way. Rules be damned. As Meyer describes Steven Jobs: "He deliberately sets out to break rules and jar people with his iconoclastic chutzpah."[3]

BrainStyle Clue:

*When dealing with a **Conceptor** expect him to "create" a decision. Ask questions about what appear to be disconnected parts of his ideas. Help draw out connections and support unformed thoughts. You can evaluate a whole decision most effectively much later, after the decision has some of its parts connected.*
For best results, refer to rules or standards only as points of reference, never as limits or gospel.

People in the **Conceptor** brainstyle continually re-define, re-sort, and re-view a problem. The left/right exchange that goes on in their brains seems to demand a constant reshaping of information. The **Conceptor** speaks of being able to arrive at a <u>number</u> of solutions to a single problem. This capacity to generate multiple solutions gives this brainstyle natural flexibility to modify, incorporate, and integrate others' ideas.

If a decision needs modifying or requires a total revision, the **Conceptor** is ready to move. After all, there is no reason to stay with a bad decision when there is another one waiting in the wings. The **Conceptor** creates broad enough decisions that specific plans of attack can be changed easily. The difference between the **Conceptor** and other brainstyles is that the **Conceptor's** strength resides here: in the inventing and generating stage. Only the **Knower** is best on the front end of a project — in a very different way.

BrainStyle Clue:

*To arrive at a decision, the **Conceptor** talks around a problem conceptually, using diagrams, metaphors, and images as support. He will probably exhibit a variety of moods — from excitement to negativity and back. He envisions several solutions and how to deliver them. But because of the speed at which passion and logic pour out, the **Conceptors'** first attempts at articulation may sound disjointed or irrelevant.*

One final word on decision making: it is important to remember that *the ability to make a decision quickly has no particular value.* Most of the things you will deal with in life that give your life quality really don't have a lot to do with doing something in a split second. What is important to recognize is that *a good decision with long-term value needs the contribution of both sides of the brain.* That's the only way it will have the flexibility it needs to deal with changes that are bound to come up. *BrainStyles* allows you to sort through the type of decision you can expect from which set of gifts. The **Conceptor** is best at coming up with "umbrella" decisions in a complex area the quickest. *He needs others to make it do-able.* The **Knower** is best at sorting complexity to a focused, logical outcome. Others can help **Knowers** see the feeling side to make the solution acceptable to other brainstyles. The leader knows he needs different views to reach a best — not a perfect — answer.

Conflict

The **Conceptor** deals with conflict as just another problem. What the **Deliberator** and the **Conciliator** define as "conflict" is merely problem-solving to the **Conceptor.** And so it appears that the **Conceptor** doesn't mind "conflict" at all. To people in this brainstyle, conflict is a part of the big picture: you have people, you have resources, you have disagreements, ideas that clash. Most **Conceptors** we have met love a good "negotiation." Karen, a young

Conceptor in her 20's was a fast track consultant with Arthur Andersen's Consulting group based on her ability to "wheel and deal" — quickly strategize — while putting together client proposals for new products. "I loved it when things got 'hot.' The tenser the better. That's when I was the most cool. I love being at the center of the storm." Yet while the **Conceptor** *feels* a great deal, and personally enters the fray, he can be done with it and move on to the next event without rancor (unlike the **Conciliator**, who takes conflict personally and has a very hard time letting go of the feelings once they're stirred up). Timing is the difference. The **Conceptor** will add left-brain logic faster than will the **Conciliator.** **Conceptors** have their eyes on winning the war against whatever blocks the way to their vision of the future. If losing this or that skirmish happens, it happens.

Compared with the **Conceptor,** other brainstyles are limited in their natural capacities to deal with conflict. The real difference is in timing, as indicated below:

•The **Knower** deals with conflict with rapid left-brain solutions. These can come across as edicts. Other brainstyles don't have time to sort out the issues. Their reactions are to get scared, be "intimidated" and either give in or resist what appear as "controls."

• The **Conciliator** tries to bring harmony, negotiate around conflict, or he becomes defensive to avoid conflict. These responses are ways of slowing down the issues to allow time for a lot of right-brain "processing."

• The **Deliberator** avoids conflict when it contains emotions because emotions do not make sense. There are **Time Zero** events in a conflict situation. This brainstyle needs to slow down the issues, sort and organize them for logical solutions.

Conflict means having to decide how a company's resources will be allocated. *It begins with setting priorities.* This rests on an ability to see the overview. The **Conceptor** can get to the key issues in a *new* area quickly. Conflict means having to fire someone who is not doing a good job. Conflict is coaching an employee to do a job that fits her brainstyle rather than one that fits her *"shoulds"* ("I should be promoted by now".) This requires focused interpersonal skills. Each of these issues requires a willingness to confront another's personal, deeply-held beliefs and agendas with reason and compassion. These issues also require that the conflict be handled in a clean and closed-ended fashion. The resentment that grows out of unsettled or suppressed conflict will prevent a business from reaching its goals. Each brainstyle will get into fights according to its area of strength, or interest. This is the most personal "turf" a person can have. And though each brainstyle will fight over all four issues, the real heart of the matter — the basic battle for each brainstyle will be in their area of strength.

- **Knowers** "fight" over who is going to *win.*
- **Conciliators** "fight" over *personal issues* or *values.*
- **Deliberators** "fight" over what is *right.*
- **Conceptors** "fight" over the *big picture,* the broader issues.

Brainstyles dictate what people fight over and how they will fight.

Case in point: Two business partners, Jim and Bill, have worked together very successfully for twenty years. One of the major factors that maintains their good relationship is the way they handle conflict. Jim, a **Conceptor,** takes the lead in confronting the broad issues between them in order to prevent quarrels based on hardened positions. Bill, a **Conciliator,** will bring up problems in Operations (his area). Jim immediately looks for the larger picture Bill's specifics can lead to in the future, and the potential for harming or helping the business *as a whole.* Bill contributes by not demanding control of how they work together. He focuses on maintaining the relationship, allowing his pushy partner to "get it all out, without me taking it personally, or even seriously. I just can't react to a lot of what Jim says. I look for what to build on." This more laid back approach is crucial to their partnership, as Jim will be the first to admit, "with someone who also needs control, we'd be fighting all the time."

A particularly touchy area has been money — especially the distribution that each takes from the partnership. Bill (the

Conciliator) mentioned several times that he was concerned about how the two of them handled expenses. Jim suggested lunch and started the conversation with "I don't want you to decide this today. But I want to look at how we share control of the company and how we make decisions."

After looking at the much larger issue of control, they proceeded to discuss the investment strategy for the next few years that Jim had been thinking of. Each item was an emotional one for both of them. Bill brought up how much they would take as salary. As Jim moved through each item with him, he kept referring back to the larger issues, looking for how he could get Bill's needs (managing operations and marketing, dealing with customers) met and feel he was fairly rewarded. They addressed salary, formalizing different roles, and a new organizational structure — after *several* discussions. The issue of expenses fell into a much broader picture, once it was established. Jim says frankly, "I just don't take it as personally as Bill. And I guess I plow through the gut issues a little quicker — they just don't bother me in the same way. I can really get upset if I can't deal with the broader issue, though. And Bill knows it. I demand a lot of control." Bill says, "He can really get me mad at first — it seems he wants to do everything his way. But once I see what he's talking about, I see the logic and we negotiate from there. He gets things going for us, no doubt about it, bringing up issues that are often painful. We make a good team because I can figure out how to get things to work at the 'nitty-gritty' level beyond his big ideas."

BrainStyle Clue:

*Although the **Conceptor** doesn't mind conflict, it may be very uncomfortable for others. A disciplined **Conceptor** can direct his energy at doing battle with issues rather than the people who propose them.*
*The mature **Conceptor** learns the difference between taking control for my goals and using control for our goals,*
SHORT TERM vs. LONG TERM WINS.

Jim, in the example above, has studied and applied the material on brainstyles to his partnership. This is not at all the case in most partnerships. In an article in *Inc.* magazine entitled "Reconcilable Differences," a different story of a partnership is presented in which a "rapid accumulation of differences and delusions forced them to scrap the company they had worked so hard to create."[4] The authors interview psychologists and business consultants to get these recommendations: 1) *stay true to the goal of minimizing emotions in favor of rational thinking* and 2) *plan around a pre-defined business concept and plan.*

If the ideas presented here so far make sense, you know by now that the first recommendation is impossible. The way to make a partnership work is to *include* the fact that one partner is more emotional, and work *that* into the execution of the business plan. The two brainstyles written about in the *Inc.* article were a **Conceptor** and a **Deliberator**. Each brainstyle had its own interpretation of the goals and the business plan. Resentments over money and clients increased and communication stopped. The *Inc.* recommendations for focus are rational, but only a start toward making the partnership work. It is not enough to focus on clear goals and communicate regularly. Partners must manage differences, as Jim and Bill demonstrate, by discussing issues using brainstyle timing as a key factor in resolving them.

Management Potential

The **Conceptor** creates the vision and then excites and invites others to take it forward. "When it comes down to it, I do one thing: I have a vision, then I create an atmosphere that involves the people in that vision." So Norman Brinker, Dallas CEO of Brinker International (the former Chili's restaurants), is quoted in the Dallas Morning News.[5] Sure, it sounds good, trendy, the right management thing to say. Does he do it? The reporter adds "His presence seems to charge the atmosphere. And he seems to draw vigor from those around him." The article lists his priorities; listening, learning from the best. "Finally, he says you have to shake things up now and again 'No matter how good your record is to date, if you continue to do that ad infinitum you're going to be second rate.'"

At all management levels, the **Conceptor** seems to have the knack of getting other people excited about his ideas. Steven Jobs has been described as *"the Electric Kool-Aid Acid Dream Machine."*⁶ Jobs is a man who offers dreams. Ted Turner of Turner Broadcasting, labeled "a zealot in search of a cause" by *The New Republic*⁷, seeks in his own idiosyncratic way to establish world peace — and build an empire on the way. Mid-level managers and school teachers who are **Conceptors** get others excited about possibilities in the future with their vision of possibilities. Other brainstyles create excitement also — differently.

The appeal of breakthrough dreamers seems to be related to the fact that the **Conceptor's** ideas are original and possibly novel — at least in the mind of the **Conceptor,** who has no patience with those who aren't equally excited about his creativity. The cockiness of this brainstyle is likely to create resentment among the **Conceptor's** peers and sounds of indignation from superiors who are policy mavens. For while the mature **Conceptor** can become a superb manager, the young one can be a trial for other brainstyles.

Consider one of Jobs' associates at Apple who told Meyer, "A lot of negative baggage comes with this guy." Meyer goes on to report that Jobs could be "perfectly charming one day and screamingly abusive another." He could walk into the middle of a meeting, listen for a moment, and then tell everyone they were all wrong, their ideas were "bullshit," and that <u>this</u> was the only way the project could go. **Conceptors** can look and act like **Knowers,** who demand things to be *one way*. The strong left and right brain is influencing the **Conceptor.** Female **Conceptors** have said they can be overly aware of others' opinions — not to the detriment of the idea — but very sensitive to others' reactions. Each has learned how to channel that **Time Zero** response into action.

When the **Conceptor** sees what must be done, he seems to fall in love with his idea, and often gets impatient with slow motion. This is a trait shared with many **Conciliators** who are fast to action.

The quick left brain directs action. Rules and gate keepers slow things up. Rules are the past and the status quo — two concepts that the **Conceptor** finds uninteresting. It is the way the **Conceptor** uses rules as mere starting blocks in his race for new adventures that people are attracted to. As the **Conceptor** and all other brainstyles realize how this works, personality will take its rightful place: behind strengths.

It is amazing that the **Conceptor** ever survives in the corporate structure long enough to rise to levels of recognized authority. In fact, many do not. Their opinions generate office politics — as do **Knowers'** stands on issues. You must be for the idea or oppose it. They leave larger firms to build their own companies. People in this brainstyle can be both excessively confident of their abilities and adaptable enough to find ways in and around the system. They thrive on challenge and cannot imagine that there is some task or problem they can't do or solve.

It may be true that the *mature* **Conceptor** is the best suited of all the brainstyles for leading, but if so, the young **Conceptor** is in trouble. Junior members of companies are supposed to follow — people <u>and</u> rules — not tell others what to do. Even when a **Conceptor** reaches an age "suitable for leading," he may run into resistance from those who expect the leader to do what he asks *others* to do. A good leader *does not operate* the team (or division, or corporation) but sees to it that *the team operates.* In the case of this brainstyle, there must be some track record so that others can support the idea — if not the person.

Throughout his career, the **Conceptor** may appear less directed and more "blue sky" than the **Knower,** less team oriented than the **Conciliator,** and less knowledgeable than the **Deliberator.** However, the flexibility of the **Conceptor's** brain process allows for appreciation of, if not understanding, of complex concepts — like music or physics or organizational systems. Unstructured projects are the **Conceptors'** playground. They "order the universe" (try to control it) by conceptualizing it into their own vision, while struggling to adjust/survive in the corporate structure. Steve Jobs did well until the corporate structure that built up around him could no longer deal with its unstructured creator who never learned to play by corporate rules. Michael Meyer reports that "according to the people around him, Steve Jobs' greatest strength is his ability to think freely, to break down assumed or conventional boundaries."[8] This kind of thinking is often visionary, providing a future direction for the rest of the team — *if they will accept it.*

Typically, people in this brainstyle have no trouble making reputations for themselves. If they are as intelligent and competent as they are confident and creative, then **Conceptors** can rise to the top and lead the way, naming new directions for everyone — including themselves — as they go.

Case in point: Doug was a young engineer employed at a major tire and rubber company. As a junior chemist with no track record, he got wind of a tire that kept falling apart in every test. Major resources were involved. The problem was one of international proportions. The company stood to lose money or its reputation if the tire continued to fail, yet no one was coming up with a solution. Doug decided it was his personal challenge.

His job did not even vaguely involve the problem area. This was the turf of the *senior* chemists, engineers, and designers. However, on his signature he could draw unmonitored funds for testing. And so Doug started his unauthorized testing — not only in his own area, but in the design area as well. He asked questions and learned the angles of the cords and how flat the tread was. Using the tire building facilities on site, he ran experiments he designed himself. He tracked them statistically, amassing his own data base. He changed the cord angles. He changed the flatness. He lined up the data, saw a new way to engineer the tire — and hid the new specifications.

While R & D was still focusing on the rubber, Doug had conclusive evidence that the tire failed because of the design. He knew absolutely how to solve the problem — and he couldn't show it to anybody. *He wasn't supposed to be working on it in the first place.*

It wasn't until there was a meeting of the company's international group that Doug had his opportunity. The tire was the topic of discussion. Its failure was still a mystery. Doug stood up — statistics in hand — and started his presentation on how to reconstruct the tire and solve the problem.

Silence.

No applause for the maverick.

Doug may have been right, but he broke all the rules.

The problem disappeared. But that was pretty much the last Doug ever heard (from management) about his work. He had to be content with a certain "underground" reputation over the next few years, and an eventual promotion into Engineering. His six-year career at the company ended with what was undoubtedly a loss for the company's growth, when he went on to bigger opportunities elsewhere.

The real shame is that large corporations don't even know what they are losing when a maverick leaves. Corporate comfort is valued over corporate entrepreneurship.

Just as the **Knower** is an individual contributor who is a natural expert, or very innovative systems manager, or a Turnaround General the **Conceptor** is most at home when leading. Seeing what to do and telling others about it comes naturally to this brainstyle (*too* naturally, some would say). **Conceptors** <u>like</u> running the show; they can be good at it.

The **Deliberator** can lead by example, with organization, planning, incremental, even dynamic, strategies that move forward logically; the **Conciliator** can generate new alternatives and ideas while bringing along the team, and the **Knower** envision applications and drive them home — but only the **Conceptor** is detached enough from yesterday's rules and conventions, while informed by today's feelings, to freely create. The detachment comes naturally because with both sides of the brain in action from **Time Zero,** the **Conceptor** does not have to reference the linear past with the left brain in order to know what to do next.

In a time of rapid transformations in the workplace, the

Conceptor can best "manage to live with chaos." A natural person for start-ups, the **Conceptor** will, we predict, be a natural leader. These strengths do not, however, predict success. These are the reasons why.

• When the **Conceptor** is working on a plan, he needs to "percolate" with others who are willing to be supportive of his idea in order to unfold it by talking it through.

• He often has "Ah-ha!" realizations alone or in conversation. He can get excited about these insights. He'll want to talk about them — maybe diagram them. They *may* lead to something wonderful, but they depend on the right data and testing.

• The **Conceptor** doesn't collect data. He gets an idea and then searches for the connections with other concepts. Data come later, and most often are accessed randomly. Collecting data is this brainstyle's *non-strength* and can best be supplied by **Knowers** and **Deliberators.**

• At first, a **Conceptor's** ideas may seem muddled and incoherent when the issue is large. For simpler problems this is not the case. These people have to tell their big ideas several times before they know *exactly* how to say *exactly* what they mean to say. The repetitions can help others understand and sign up for the program. This takes time.

• For the **Conceptor,** there is no idea or plan so good that it can't be changed — even his own. This means a flexibility that opens possibilities. However, these ideas and their revisions need to be limited: by time, by available resources. Overcommitment to too many new ideas will limit effectiveness and overburden those who get delegated to.

Delegation

The **Conceptor** delegates well.

His preference is to start things. His non-strength is execution. Early on he may sound like one who is simply getting everyone else to do the dog work. As he matures, he needs to truly delegate in a way that values the expertise of others. As Henry Ford once said, "I don't have to know the answer. I just have to know who to call."

Once it becomes clear to the **Conceptor** that his gift involves looking to the future and seeing what the possibilities are, he stops making excuses for not following through and ensures his "non-strength" (following up) will be covered by support systems and those who are naturals at running the plan. He also learns that no one can execute an idea as fast as he can come up with them. The effective **Conceptor** learns to discipline his own timing of new projects and ideas, the ineffective **Conceptor** does not.

Case in Point: Bob, a **Conceptor** in his early forties, was on the fast track in a specialty chemical firm. He was dynamic — great with ideas and people. Put in charge of a new acquisition, Bob had a number of ideas about how to move things faster and more effectively to new profitability. Within six months he instituted two major reorganizations, one of which moved the field marketing offices. Any change is disruptive. Bob followed one change with another and didn't get *input from the team.* Accounts were scrambled and sales lost. Too much, too soon. The **Conceptor** outpaced the execution which was deadly for the organization. He got the ideas himself and told the marketers. He needed to spend time helping the organization follow through on one change at a time — offering his flexibility and vision to the problems that arose. He needed a dialogue. Instead, his timing was off. The marketing group stopped listening to his "idea for the day." He lost credibility within the team. Then he lost his job. A **Conceptor** will never be as good as the **Deliberator** at executing an idea or as adept as the Knower in "cutting to the chase." And for all of his people skills, he will not have the **Conciliator's** gift of building the relationships once the goal has been defined. Once the **Conceptor** has determined: "There is where we will camp," he might easily forget to pack the tent poles, gas the car, or check with the Park Service to make sure there's space. He delegates those parts of the trip to others. Relieved of the chore of picking the destination, those with other gifts can determine what's needed to get there in style.

Case in point: To contrast with Bob, "Trammell Crow, America's biggest landlord and one of its richest men, started out 40 years ago building warehouses. Crow's informal management style — intuitively picking a partner here, a partner there — allowed him to build his vast real-estate empire." So starts the cover article "The *Real* Art of the Deal" in *Inc.* magazine in November of 1988. The story of Crow's life, and realizing his vision ('He wanted to build a company that would be the IBM of the real estate industry'), is the story of a man who set his own rules and *trusted* others to carry them forward, that is, he put his vision first before anything, including his own personal control. Very radical in any business — but especially in the real estate business.

What stands out in Trammell Crow's case is his willingness to lead the way in building the company — including getting himself out of the way so that execution wasn't his main responsibility. Crow explains, 'You've got to know and remember that this company wasn't made by me, but by Don and Joel — and 100 others.' The dialogue was continual between chief and followers.

It is important to point out here that the **Conceptor's** capacity — even necessity — for invention does not make this brainstyle better, smarter, or more accomplished than other brainstyles. It simply means that the gift of rapid left/right brain exchange carries with it the ability to make something out of nothing in the future: to create. A **Conceptor's** brainstyle seeks to change things, whether things need changing or not. This is a very different process from the **Deliberator's** rational, usually diplomatic, innovation: making something out of something — e.g., improving, or making what exists better. The **Conciliator's** imaginative brainstorming also relies on what is already there, as does the **Knower's** decision-making. The **Conceptor** alone can naturally start from scratch. And as you can see, this is the good news and the bad news for this brainstyle.

> *BrainStyle Clue:*
>
> *If the **Deliberator's** motto is "If it ain't broke, don't fix it," and the **Knower** says, "You break it, and I'll break you!" then the **Conceptor's** motto is, "Let's break it and fix it, and then maybe break it again."*
> *[The **Conciliator** has no mottos that include the word "break" except "Let's take a break" or "Breakin' up is Hard To Do."]*

Where others are content (a *dreadful* thing for the changer), the **Conceptor** sees problems that need fixing. He is beset by what in the artist would be called "divine discontent." Meyer reports that "One body of opinion suggests that Turner grabbed MGM not merely to get new programming for TBS, but simply to do it. To get on to something bigger and better, to create new challenges."[9]

> *BrainStyle Clue:*
>
> *A **Conceptor** has the strengths to see that the system operates by:*
> * *establishing the game (overviews),*
> * *setting up the boundaries (strategies and limits),*
> * *confronting those who want to play outside of them (handling conflict), and*
> * *negotiating agreements where every person can win within the game.*

The brainstyle strengths of the **Conceptor** fit the criteria. The variables are self-esteem and maturity level.

Learning

The **Conceptor** captures unfixed concepts that gather shape and coherence from the left-brain/right-brain exchange. More than any other brainstyle, the **Conceptor** needs to deal with information in overviews, punchlines or summaries, or have the time to create them from a few key facts. This often means visual or verbal presentations. In fact, learning seems to occur for these people when they have a forum in which to articulate and thrash out ideas. As a result of their need to "talk through an idea," **Conceptors** are not always popular with teachers. Yet they flourish when challenged and praised. All in all, formal education for students in this brainstyle can be a frustrating ordeal — for everyone. They are just not very good at sitting still and learning what is put before them.

Conceptors don't like doing their homework. As a rule, they don't like to sit still and read. They hate detailed analysis and reporting. *They get the drift.* They like restating or summarizing in their own way. (They may have this in common with some of each of the other brainstyles who will act similarly but for their <u>own</u> reasons.) They resist discipline.

For the **Conceptor,** individual facts or details do not become a part of memory until *after* she has stored entire concepts that have been formed through the left-brain/right-brain process. Moreover, **Conceptors** *store only those details that support the concepts they see as important.* That's because the details have no special significance in themselves until they have been blended into the "big picture" that the **Conceptor** can give you complete.

As students, **Conceptors** may "test high," that is, they do not show up as very bright until they take tests, applying their ideas. It may not be uncommon for the "lazy" one of the class to score in the 90+ percentile. In class these people may not participate the way "bright ones" do.

People in other brainstyles, particularly the **Deliberator** (the detail memorizer, or "bright one"), are likely to take the **Conceptors'** generalizations as sloppy thinking or, worse, manipulation of the facts to reach their own conclusions. The linear logic and clear explanations are missing. The **Conceptor** seems to discover his own meanings as he talks. This is because the right brain has a big part in his thinking and it <u>often</u> becomes clear when spoken by the left brain. The **Conceptor** learns best by talking things through.

Put a **Conceptor** in front of a blackboard with a piece of chalk in his hand, and then get ready to go tripping. The **Conceptor** learns most quickly at the head of a conversation with those who are willing to go on a freewheeling ride through a world of ideas. **Conceptors** *are active, fast learners.* The more the **Conceptor** scribbles and talks and charts about what he is thinking, the more he learns what he is thinking about. The more participative classrooms of the last few years have discovered how discussions and experienced-based learning works well for some and not others. Using brainstyles as a way to structure learning groups could promote more efficient learning for everyone.

> *BrainStyle Clue:*
>
> *The **Conceptor** stores concepts, not information. As a result, he will often slow down a process of information delivery so he has time mentally to build a concept around a fact. This process sounds like interrupting. It is. But unless he interrupts, the **Conceptor** will lose interest or become disruptive.*

This method of learning, opposite to that of the model **Deliberator,** does not fit our expectations or administrations. **Conceptors** can be "late bloomers," who learn rules of social etiquette later in life.

Risk Taking

Each brainstyle takes "risks" in its area of strength. Onlooking brainstyles label such actions as "risks," but the person doing the risking rarely sees things that way. They are merely "problem solving."

From the outside, **Conceptors** look as if they are addicted to risk. They appear to consider only projects filled with the dangers of the unknown. In fact, **Conceptors** consider many more sides of a project than the spontaneous, impatient **Conciliator.** The **Conceptor** who doesn't allow her own brain speed to run away with her takes in other ideas before committing everything to a project.

The **Conceptor** loves the unknown. "I'm at my <u>best</u> in a new situation" was said by several **Conceptors** in interviews. The risks taken are generally calculated risks, based on an assessment of what the future could be like if certain things can be done. In their own minds, **Conceptors** have determined the questions that need answers. These questions can produce a "Go" or "No Go" with the authority of reason and feeling combined. The "risks" so apparent to other styles are manageable problems to be solved, instantly, over and over, for the **Conceptor.**

By the time the **Conceptor** says, "Go," it is likely that she has on hand more than one arrow for her bow, not to mention plans for containment and damage control should the project go bust. If Plan A fails or runs into trouble, there are always Plan B and Plan C, strung and ready for action. As a result, the **Conceptor** is prepared to change course at a moment's notice without having to stop and begin all over again. Unlike the **Knower,** who can lock onto a decision as final, definitive, and unalterable, or the **Deliberator,** who has labored to arrive at one and is reluctant to change, the **Conceptor** begins a project with two back-up solutions and so is able to change on the fly.

It is the *calculated* quality of the more disciplined **Conceptor's** risk-taking that separates people in this brainstyle into capable visionaries or "gamblers" and "prophets." The **Conceptor** brainstyle can make no pretensions to being able to predict what the future will be. Some may decide to do so. The strength of this brainstyle is to look at problems and envision a future state, complete with feelings and results. The end is created from a series of solutions, and is charged with the **Conceptor's** personal confidence that his problem-solving ability will make the idea successful on the way. It must be added that the difference between a **Knower** and a **Conceptor** in the life of a risky project is the part that emotions play. **Conceptors** are very open to the input from the right brain. A great deal of anxiety, worry, sensitivity to other's warnings about problems will be major factors for **Conceptors**, taken very personally. A **Conceptor** will bring a great deal of passion to a risky venture. A **Knower** will bring a great deal of drive and logic.

Case in point: David, a **Conceptor,** and co-author of this book, managed a specialty plastics manufacturing subsidiary for a large corporation. Consultants were hired to assess the business potential of this operation and predicted only marginal success at best. After an entire career working inside corporations, David found the idea of taking over a poorly run business and making it profitable a risk he was very excited about. He started out envisioning everything that could go right.

Within six months of purchase, all equipment broke down, idling a three-shift production operation. Interest rates on the cash that was keeping the company afloat went to 24 percent. Product that was shipped was returned. His personal life was where he expressed his anxieties — sleepless nights and high tension. David's response at work to an increasingly difficult situation: work on the few things you could fix, that would give the biggest payoff, and let the rest go (clarifying priorities). While shut down, David focused on negotiating prices for raw materials that were low enough to give the company an edge. He worked on formulating products that would resolve field problems. And he channeled his feelings into support for the employees. He became a cheerleader for his people, who were very skeptical about keeping their jobs in what looked to be a very shaky company. "I let about a million things go and concentrated everything on these three," he reported. He showed up in the plant at 4 a.m. He worked with maintenance with sleeves rolled up to unclog pipes. He worked with his direct reports on teamwork. Keep afloat. Attend to people. The creditors said it was a very risky venture but, with the plans working, continued the funding. There were so <u>many</u> problems that only continual sorting and re-emphasizing direction carried the day. Those who knew of the problems said the risks were enormous.

The **Conceptor** strategized to get to daylight just over the horizon. The manufacturing company built and maintained market dominance. The ingredients: enormous teamwork, pricing, and product formulation that made the customer happy. The driving force: a vision of what success would look like in both global <u>and</u> everyday terms.

BrainStyle Clue:

Conceptors *may sound arrogant and be "blue sky." Look beneath all the swagger for the basics: competence and soundness of the plan. What would it cost to get to their vision of the future? Provide boundaries and benchmarks to discipline the process they use.*

If Tom Peters had his way, this "do it, fix it, try it" brainstyle would be much more numerous in corporate America. The problem is that the corporate world is set up for more orderly practices and procedures. The few **Conceptors** there are are more likely to leave to start small companies.

Chapter Five

The Conciliator

CHAPTER FIVE

THE CONCILIATOR

kon sil´ ē ā ter: [a person who]
overcomes distrust or hostility;
placates, wins over, brings together.

For the **Conciliator,** the response from the right brain is immediate. The logical, left-brain response is delayed. As a result, action is impulsive and spontaneous. Later, the left brain judges and organizes the initial reaction.

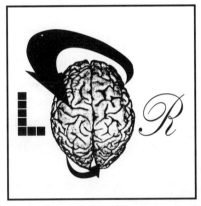

The gift of this brainstyle is to bring the full force of the right brain to a situation. The right brain is the side that sees no distinctions, no time nor measures by which to judge. It looks out past the language of the left brain for unity, harmony and meaning, to form relationships. It senses, empathizes and bonds. This brainstyle is a natural to bring feeling and meaning to the logic of the linear.

In the data base of over 600 people observed for brainstyle, we found 34% of them to be this right-brainstyle. Of these, roughly half are male and half are female.

More than any other brainstyle, the **Conciliator** seems to seek *comfort.* As the right brain looks for synthesis, convergence or similarities, this brainstyle seeks to create relationships with others so all will be in harmony (everyone is *comfortable*) in their world. **Conciliator's** apply their strengths most naturally with people in groups, teams, or with friends as they bring people together in alliances or working toward mutual goals. "Comfort" is when right brains are in sync — without words, yet with an understanding, a bond. The tolerant Conciliator has the best chance of encouraging people to be comfortable working together and *liking* one another. In business **Conciliators** naturally like working with people, supporting and being supported by relationships. Work is often *family,* clients are *friends,* customers are special to the right-brained **Conciliator.**

Decision Making

The **Conciliator** makes quick decisions based on feelings — subject to revision. On any given issue, the **Conciliator** will likely make two decisions, not just one. The instinctive response at **Time Zero** to a request or demand for a decision pours out of the right brain and aims to please. Left without the critical influence of the left brain, the feeling, right brain response wants to say "Yes!" and often does.

The difficulty is that once the structure-bearing left brain has a chance to catch up with the spontaneous right, the decision gets modified. At **Time Zero** the **Conciliator** responds with, "Sure, I can do that." At **Time Zero** + **X** (maybe as soon as an hour later), the **Conciliator** may re-decide, "That's a bad idea." As a result, the **Conciliator** — the great doer, organizer, consensus builder — is often regarded as indecisive or, worse, undependable: "They say one thing and then go in another direction 24 hours later!"

The mirror image of the **Knower** who makes a quick, left-brain decision and sticks to it (the right brain input that comes later only serves to support the "logical" conclusion), the **Conciliator** comes up with an initial decision based on <u>feelings</u>, then rounds up all the facts to back up the initial reaction. To become disciplined, the **Conciliator** has to work for a more balanced decision. He just needs to hold off on making that first, quick non-decision until the left brain has had a chance to enter and put pure feeling in balance with reason. Timing becomes particularly important for the **Conciliator** as he makes decisions — especially major decisions concerning life plans and long-range goals.

In working with other brainstyles on new decisions requiring a lot of left-brain facts or structure, the **Conciliator** may feel and appear "slower." The brainstyle strength is contributing rapidly to possibilities or future applications — often freely associated. The right-brain input is much greater for the **Conciliator,** hence less logical and more in need of sorting and organizing against a task and within boundaries. The many decisions of the **Conceptor** can be distracting and disruptive to the main job of the **Conciliator:** putting words to feelings or hunches. The **Knower's** fast logic doesn't even take the right brain into account. Brainstyle timing is of the essence, then, in optimizing different strengths. The **Conciliator** can easily be left behind in a **Time Zero** discussion in which fast logical decisions are imperative. What a **Conciliator** *can* do is give quick reactions and ideas. Logical decisions need preparation. Knowing that timing is key and strengths are different can make all the difference.

Case in point: Steve is a manager of distribution for a major soft drink company. In a planning meeting he was pressed by his boss to come up with new shipping routes. Before that moment, Steve had never thought about coming up with new routes. He was faced with a **Time Zero** event.

True to his **Conciliator** brainstyle, he reacted emotionally: "We can't do it. No way." Later, after cooling off and giving himself a chance to let his left brain get into the action, Steve was able to come up with several options for new routes. "I just didn't like the pressure," he admitted, "and I guess I flew off the handle a bit. I work a lot better when I have more time to think about things."

While it is true that **Conciliators** like to say "Yes" to most requests and thereby avoid conflict, when pressured — and desiring to look as tough as the next guy — they are just as likely to lash out with a changeable "No," a "No" that can reverse as quickly as a positive response.

Steve now asks for a break for a few minutes when meetings get tense or emotional for him. "When I feel comfortable, I perform better and give a lot more to the meeting. And I don't just react, as in the past. I let the first response 'sit there' until I can see some alternatives. It's working well for me and my peers."

BrainStyle Clue:

Conciliators *need time to "think about it" — whether they know it or not. If you want a final decision or a true commitment from a* **Conciliator,** *don't ask for an immediate response. A* **Conciliator** *decision made under pressure is too fluid to depend on. The* **Conciliator** *needs to figure out how the thing can be accomplished. Once that's clear, the decision is made.*

Conciliators do not perform well in new areas (make reliable, new decisions) under pressure, especially time pressure.

As with every rule there appear to be exceptions. This is the difference you must learn in applying *The BrainStyles System™:* you must look past appearances to **Time Zero,** as well as a pattern over time.

In brainstyle interviews, there is a pattern shown by **Conciliators** in regard to decision-making that causes confusion. Described as "stubborn, quick decision-makers who need a lot of control," only an interview about *first* responses to *new* situations off the job surfaced the more right-brained natural response. Jim, 29, Bill, in his late 40's, along with Wendell, (also in his 40's mentioned in Chapter One) are three examples of men who have learned a set of technical skills — accounting, technical drafting, and manufacturing — and, in working in those areas come up with rapid decisions which they will not change easily. Each of these men have been described as **Knowers** by those who work with them: either they are tough or they are tender. This is what opposite brainstyles have in common — either the right or the left side of the brain processing leads their actions, so they look like people of extremes. **Knowers** and **Conciliators** <u>can</u> <u>look</u> <u>alike</u>! The difference between these three men and Bo, Kevin or Fran, natural **Knowers,** is this: The **Conciliators** get an image, an intuition or a feeling response first, then they attack a task. The **Conciliators** all feel most comfortable, and are at their <u>best</u>, working with others, though they have chosen jobs — even careers — where the daily emphasis is to solve left-brained problems and design and implement solutions. Each has *decided* (stored in memory) that "changing your mind is wishy-washy" — not what a strong person/leader does. They each admit to being stubborn. They have *learned to adapt* to hard-edged situations by putting feelings in support of their decisions — and so they stick to their idea in the face of disagreement — at a certain price: "I guess I explode sometimes because I have a lot of feelings on a subject," says Wendell, who admits to needing to learn to control his temper. Better that he focused on his feelings *as an asset.*

In contrast, Bo, the entrepreneur and turn-around specialist, Kevin, an engineer, and Fran, currently a painter, all make very clear, factual decisions — usually about how to "win" the sale or the argument first and turn to relationships or feelings later, and to a lesser degree. They do not put the "stubborn" or defensive feelings behind decisions nearly as often. They are just certain, factual — logical. First comes the structure, the quick analysis in a very impersonal way — *even about very personal subjects.* Fran says about her portraits and realistic paintings,

> "I have to get the business out of the way first, then I can have fun painting. It's no good if you never get paid — even though I don't always [get paid]. I get involved with the people side <u>later</u>."

None of the **Knowers** mentioned have chosen careers where

forming and keeping relationships are critical to success, (in their view). When Kevin applies his expertise to projects in the telecommunications area, he certainly must sell his ideas and influence others. Both he and Bo talk first of bringing efficiency, influencing others with their results. Relating to others is something they "work on" or "have learned to do." Both **Knowers** say this about tasks they know well — not new situations. Even Fran, a former flight attendant, "brought more efficiency to the job than making friends just for the sake of making friends."

BrainStyle Clue:

Conciliators *can look like* **Knowers** *in areas they know well. The feelings inform the decision and make it stick. To get them unstuck, talk about the larger purpose of the project. Help the* **Conciliator** *define his own personal meaning for goals. Get him feedback from others. Show him how his single solution makes others feel uncomfortable. A* **Conciliator** *will understand. Then you can re-start the project using others' input and the strength of the* **Conciliator** *at getting others involved.*

Conflict

Conflict, in everyday terms, involves discomfort, disharmony, and **Time Zero** decisions. These are non-strengths of this brainstyle. Emotional or intuitive responses are the strength. To most **Conciliators,** the first reaction they have to left-brain judgments or strong emotion directed at them is the perception that they are being "attacked". They then defend. The most important thing for this brainstyle to recognize is that they have an instantaneous response, and, rather than attempt to learn not to have one, to focus the one they have. Or have the reaction and delay the words about it. The good news and the bad news for the **Conciliator** is that they *personalize* information. In conflict this tends to slow the process of reaching a solution.

A **Conciliator** would rather lie than get involved in a conflict situation. As a builder of consensus, she takes conflict as an invalidation of everything she does well. The managers in this brainstyle are deeply invested in how people feel about doing their work. Somehow, conflict is a sure signal that the **Conciliator** has failed to communicate or to understand well enough. It is easy to see how a "tough" **Conciliator** can avoid all conflict by stubbornly defending and sticking with a decision.

Rather than deal with a situation that she cannot cure through good will, the **Conciliator** will go along with a decision she disagrees with or will fail to give critical feedback to another who has made a mistake that must be corrected. In the matter of going along, the **Conciliator** may say, "Yes," and then go off in another direction as if she had never heard the order in the first place. As for giving feedback that is not positive, the **Conciliator** may prefer to "fix it herself" (stay in control) rather than confront the one who got it wrong to correct the mistake.

The **Conciliator** uses personal influence to short-circuit conflict. This brainstyle is the master of influencing others to arrive at consensus without conflict. Other brainstyles, particularly the **Knower** and the **Conceptor,** may use confrontation to get their way or to get to the truth — or both. Not the **Conciliator.** Meeting, discussing, building rapport are the tools of the **Conciliator's** strength. The ever-present and unstated motivation of the **Conciliator** is to use this strength for harmonizing.

No other brainstyle has the natural ability to "read" more accurately and respond more immediately to a human situation than the **Conciliator**. *Intuition* is an "immediate knowing of the environment" according to brain researcher Robert Ornstein, and the right brain is the source of intuition at **Time Zero** for this brainstyle. (Intuition does not include the left-brain interpretation that occurs after the "reading"; the interpretation may not be accurate at all.) The **Conciliator** takes a very personal interest in knowing what other people need in order to feel good about a decision.

For example, Bill, a very successful sales manager, was very surprised to learn that he was the only one on his staff who naturally "reads" body language. The **Conciliator** in a meeting is able to know or sense what everybody else in the room *feels* about the subject at hand. With this immediate and continual supply of incoming data, it is often hard to keep focused on the task at hand. This can explain the inconsistent behavior of **Conciliators:** "too tough or too soft," as one CEO described his **Conciliator** plant manager. The man was reacting to constant feelings — alternately tough then kind. Policies and discipline were inconsistent.

When the **Conciliator** is leading a meeting, the most obvious, yet the most neglected, thing to do is to *prepare* for *decisions*. **Time Zero** is a time of spontaneous reaction for the **Conciliator.** This is where inconsistency comes from for this brainstyle. To talk through possible reactions of others is an excellent way to make the event a **Time Zero** + 1. Good meeting structure, e.g., meeting goal, agenda items for decision, a process for discussion, is an enormous support for this brainstyle and will put him in a position to listen and facilitate a consensus much more effectively. Short meetings on the same subject can help the imaginative **Conciliator** re-think the continual options that he thinks of and focus in on one.

Another use of **Conciliator** skills is to seek out the opinions of others, and formulate his own presentation to reflect a consensus point of view. **Conciliators** who have built on this strength have generally prepared themselves by lobbying for their position ahead of time to neutralize the opposition (and confrontation). The **Conciliator** is the natural networker and politician, and depending on the values he has decided on, either a "constructive" (longer-term, more mature) or "destructive" (short-term, self-centered, immature) influence on the team.

The **Conciliator** seeks consensus in a way unique among brainstyles. The **Knower** will come to a meeting armed with the facts and figures necessary to "nail down" a decision or blow away the opposition. Although he seeks it, consensus is not part of the

Knower's working vocabulary. The **Conceptor** will arrive with a vision and then work with others on how to get there. The **Deliberator** looks for a synthesis of ideas, often in support of a unilateral decision already prepared. The **Conciliator** looks for personal reasons, needs, as well as others' agendas. Discussion in these circumstances can elicit more participation, emotion, and alternatives than a **Deliberator's** rational, more linear approach. It also can get off the subject. Goals must be kept in focus for the participation to produce the kind of commitments that will move the group forward.

Case in point: Dan, a **Conciliator** who knows how to use his strengths, is the product manager for a plastics firm. He is ideal for this job because he has the gift of understanding, accepting, and influencing people who see things differently than he does.

Part of Dan's responsibility is to coordinate information and keep it flowing among individuals involved in sales, finance, and technical research. People in these areas have their own "language" and their own ways of getting the job done. Asking a salesman who thinks "customer!" to agree with the financial director who thinks "cost!" to agree with the technician who thinks "product!" holds great potential for all kinds of disagreement.

On those occasions when Dan has to call for a formal meeting to set a course of action, he follows a procedure he designed to reduce potential conflict.

• He meets participants one-on-one well in advance of the meeting.

• He sounds out all the players to get a feel for their personal agendas.

• He tries to influence each individual toward an alignment.

• He arrives at the meeting well-prepared and knowing pretty much what to expect.

Once the meeting starts, Dan has one more hurdle. Contrary to his urge to summarize and pull together a consensus for a quick and well-orchestrated conclusion, he has to force himself to hold back and observe the group dynamics at work. Earlier in his career, he reports, he tried to "structure every minute" and move the group along. Now he tries to bring out more open dialogue and build on what people say.

All people have some need to control. *How* they do it — what the right and left brain give them to work with — is what we observe as a "brainstyle." Dan works with "group dynamics" — how people *relate* in the *present* moment — his brainstyle strength. Without self awareness, Dan used his strengths to control the group. This is the same for all brainstyles. The choice is whether to serve yourself or use your strengths to serve others.

Just for the sake of comparison, here is how other brainstyles can conduct the same meeting:

The **Knower** comes in with a clear agenda and takes control, clarifying issues with priorities, deciding conflicts, and moving to a quick conclusion. At meeting's end, he will have formulated a clear plan of action.

The **Conceptor** sends a burst of personally exciting ideas ricocheting around the room, heats up the discussion and raises the energy level of all assembled. Controlling the pace, he may ask those attending to come back with plans to support the big picture generated in the meeting.

The **Deliberator** arrives with a list of items. The most natural product of a brainstyle that processes information so readily is to consider discussions and information-sharing the most important activity to be engaged in. All items have importance. Priority is difficult to determine. New projects are updated and milestones measure what seems to other brainstyles endless dialogue in search of the perfect decision. Urgency is continually balanced by a need for thoroughness and accuracy. Decisions are on small items. The **Deliberator** can measure success in quantity of tasks handled.

Conciliators can structure a meeting with the best of them. However, their natural bent is to "wing it" — "go with the flow." They can focus a consensus by knowing each person's personal agenda. Applying their strengths means designing meetings to promote interaction, generate ideas, and prevent conflict. Watch out for losing the focus on the goal and keeping on schedule. Left-brain measures can get away from this right-brainstyle.

Don't assume that a **Conciliator** will never fight just because he prefers to avoid conflict. Hell hath no fury like a **Conciliator** who is fed up with putting his right brain on hold for too long. Feelings have a logic of their own, especially on issues held dear or values close to the **Conciliator's** heart. When resentments get stored away, when others don't attend to feelings as well as the **Conciliator** would, the volcano may explode. Out pours the passion of the past — all freshly felt in the present moment. Personal convictions will be fought for. **Conciliators** are fierce warriors — slow to ignite, slow to calm once on fire.

> *BrainStyle Clue:*
>
> *Help the right-brainstyle stop storing up feelings: ask the* **Conciliator** *how she feels. Allowing short outbursts prevents forest fires.*

Remember, conciliating is based on heightened sensitivity.

Management

Having a **Conciliator** for a manager can be a rewarding experience, particularly if you value being part of a team, and providing the particular **Conciliator** is aware that he or she has a natural gift for noticing and responding to everything. No other brainstyle will be more generous in giving feedback for all jobs — well done, or not. Although less likely to give the negatives (anticipating what you might want to hear), the brainstyle is a continual awareness-reaction machine. The tendency is to get caught up in the details of how things are going. Thus it is essential that the company's priorities — the vision, the mission, the overall direction — must be clear for him to implement (to keep on track and enroll support for).

As long as your team has a clear vision of its future, the **Conciliator** couldn't be better at giving you the support to get there. On the other hand, if the priorities are vague or shifting, the **Conciliator** may not be very helpful. This brainstyle does not *readily see* where to go in the long term — that takes more left-brain input, over time. Both **Knowers** and **Conceptors** look ahead with more clarity than do **Conciliators.** The **Conciliator** brings meaning, personal dedication, and commitment to the job by making long-term company goals very personal for himself and his people. He does <u>not</u> come up with the goals in new areas. As one new **Conciliator** vice president put it, "We're working on the right values, and struggling a bit to hit profit targets. Our people are *involved* and *cared for.* Focus will emerge over time." The VP is well-liked, though described as confusing (when he talks about the job priorities). Meeting profit targets is more difficult than establishing rapport for this brainstyle.

BrainStyle Clue:

*When asking a **Conciliator** to lead, be sure you ask for what he can deliver. The **Conciliator** is a builder, not an architect. He comes through best when plans are well defined. Where there is no context, the **Conciliator** can procrastinate, get distracted, want to discuss the process right up to the deadline, and take a long time to bring in results. The right brain is not disciplined.*

One reason the **Conciliator** is a good manager for the good employee is that he himself hates to be managed — when this means being told what to do and how to do it. What the **Conciliator** wants is support. Personal support. He thrives on being listened to, praised, and encouraged. **Conciliators** require "high maintenance." They also provide it to others.

When put in a management position, the **Conciliator** is a great builder and healer of old wounds. So why don't **Conciliators** rise to the top of all corporations, using their supportiveness and intuition to keep industry humming along? Business by definition is a breeding ground for conflict and change — neither of which is managed particularly well by one who quickly and keenly senses the problems and adds personal meaning. The **Conciliator** is a barometer that cannot read itself. The result: **Conciliators** are found most often in the middle of large companies.

In short, the **Conciliator** manages as he would like to be managed: with praise, listening, attending to feelings. Asking the **Conciliator** for constructive criticism will keep the working relationship free of the resentments the **Conciliator** hesitates to share for fear of creating conflict.

Case in point: John joined the company as a mail clerk right out of the Marines. From the mail room, he worked his way up through production, logistics, and a variety of other jobs before arriving as VP for human resources at a major chemical company. He brought to his job a tough yet reassuring brainstyle for dealing with people. Never a technical manager in this technical company, he was someone who could put people together to get a job done.

At the time John arrived, the department had just been reorganized. Many people had been fired, and morale was low. His job was to come in to rebuild and strengthen a department that was fragmented and without direction.

What John did was settle the situation by taking three steps: (1) he surveyed the department's "customers" to find out what was needed; (2) he formulated a simple, understandable direction that reflected the larger company goals, and then (3) he built teams and coalitions.

Once the department had been reformed as a working operation, he networked outside it in an effort to restore its credibility and reputation, and inside it to build teamwork and respect among peers.

More projects of larger impact were initiated and followed through by subordinates under his guidance than in the previous decade. Conflicts between sections were addressed by using outside consultants in a "team building" session. John followed up the confrontations brought out in the offsite session with more personal support. His brainstyle management was a good "fit" for the situation: people-building rather than confrontation or creation of a new direction.

Delegation

The **Conciliator** does not delegate <u>new</u> projects easily; it's too personal. After some experience has been stored, it may be easier. Like all other processes, delegation for the **Conciliator** begins in feelings or in feeling-based memory. How difficult it is to give up control — as good delegation requires — when the attachment to that control lies in the feeling side of the brain that "knows but doesn't speak."

Under the friendly or informal handshake lies a great need for control and structure. After all, it takes time for the **Conciliator** to attach left-brain conclusions and reasons to right brain feelings. And once logic has bonded to feeling, the reasoning for action has been marked PERSONAL.

So what does right-brain feeling have to do with delegation? Everything. All projects have emotional meaning for the **Conciliator.** Everything is personal to the **Conciliator.** These people search for meaning in work, form attachments easily and don't like a great deal of change. So delegating a project — or even a piece of one — is a very personal issue.

In contrast to the **Deliberator,** who has trouble delegating because nobody else is smart enough to get it right, the **Conciliator** hesitates to delegate because nobody else will care enough. As a result, for the **Conciliator** <u>trust</u> becomes the central factor in delegation. Trust can be a heavy burden for the one entrusted with a task in the **Conciliator's** name. And even with the trust factor firmly established, it is likely that the **Conciliator** will not be able to resist "casually" checking in, just to see "how things are going." If the one delegated to do the job doesn't come through, the failure can be felt as rejection or even betrayal.

Case in point: When Joe worked with his secretary, it was enormously frustrating for him. He was as pleasant and personal as he could be in assigning work to her. In fact, he often worded his requests as "favors": "Could you do me a favor and get this out right away?"

Yet as considerate as he was to her, Joe's secretary often put off his work. He would show his annoyance and let her know that he was *hurt* by her lack of concern for his projects — and, by extension, hurt by her lack of concern for *him*. He still ended up having to do a lot of the work himself.

After Joe learned about brainstyles, he realized that in delegating he had left out the specific details regarding project priority and time schedule: both left-brain functions. As a result, every request was only a personal one, *separate from the work* his secretary did, so she put it off.

When it comes to "getting the job done," favors (and good guys) get tended to last — and maybe not at all. Recognizing their strengths, **Conciliators** need to be aware of how they communicate their feelings, and be able to separate business from the friendship, the task from the attachment to it.

BrainStyle Clue:

*When you have been delegated a task by a **Conciliator**, keep in mind that you have accepted a precious responsibility. Reassure by keeping in touch. Give feedback. Explain that you understand the **Conciliator's** sense of the project's value. Then <u>do</u> it.*

Conciliators live by the Golden Rule: Do unto others as you would have them do unto you. The best way to deal with them is to know they expect reciprocity ("I listen to him. He should listen to me.") Clarify expectations for what they mean by being "fair" (a favorite word for treating them according to their own personal standards.) Each brainstyle expects others to treat them the same way their own brainstyle does. This seems especially true for the brainstyle that is so aware of feelings and relationships.

Learning

The **Conciliator** learns by storing experiences and their meanings.

He learns especially well on two fronts: from books and experts. People in this brainstyle are often voracious readers. They read for inspiration. They read fast. And while they cannot recall the specific details of what they have read (in fact, they are notoriously bad with this kind of recall) they can come up with a good rendition of the main idea. Like the **Knower,** the **Conciliator** files in conclusions, except that **Conciliator** conclusions make *emotional* rather than logical sense.

When it comes to reading, **Conciliators** do not store information "as is" in memory the way it was written. Nor do they store concepts as the **Conceptor** does. Instead, this brainstyle must relate the information to a familiar experience: "Something like this happened to me (or I can imagine it happening)." Once he has made the personal connection, the information can go into memory. Then when it is time to be recalled, the whole package comes back up, personal experience and all.

The **Conciliator** appears to grasp new ideas more slowly than others in different brainstyles do. That's because the **Conciliator** is personalizing every major piece of data (memory games and visual cues work well for this brainstyle). They do not file information logically. Thus it is often hard to remember. The right brain has a seemingly "random access" retrieval system. Facts and stories "pop out of nowhere." This method of learning (storing, filing and retrieving) makes people in this brainstyle gifted teachers and presenters. They have an uncanny ability to make even dry facts (at least the ones they can recall) seem interesting and accessible — something you can relate to.

The other source of learning for the **Conciliator,** and perhaps the preferred source, is others. Unlike reading, talking with others provides an instant personal experience to bond with the information. The highly energetic **Conciliator** is always looking for and learning what will work with the most people.

On any given topic, the **Conciliator** is likely to have a network of people who are experts on the subject. Because the **Conciliator** is so skilled at establishing a rapport with a great variety of people, he can rapidly come up with answers and information on a variety of subjects from his personal network. His approach is a personal one. **Deliberators** are also excellent at collecting and managing resource networks, but only a few are close *friends*. With apparent effortlessness, the **Conciliator** considers a network of experts to be personal friends.

Like the **Conceptor,** the **Conciliator** *learns* by teaching, often understanding what was a vague right-brain feeling as he forces it into words. These people are wonderful actors, and natural communicators. The drive to communicate is both to influence others <u>and</u> to gain their *own* insights into what they *know* (what is stored in the right half of the brain, which has no words).

It may appear confusing as you watch how the **Conciliator** learns: "slow" to pick up new ideas and "fast" to generate reactions and imaginative — sometimes disconnected — alternatives. Which are they? Fast or slow? And do you then judge them as *smart* or *stupid* or *scatter-brained?* **Left-brain measures don't apply to the right-brain answer:**

• The **Conciliator** needs time to process *new* left-brain information through the right brain. The associations and feelings of the non-linear right brain bring many things to a financial statement, for example. When part of that statement is a **Time Zero** event, time is needed to sort through the "implications." If speed is desired, homework is required. If structure and logic are required, it will only be in an area of the **Conciliator's** expertise and experience.

• The **Conciliator** is fastest at dumping out right-brain images with no strings attached. In artistic or creative settings he will pour forth <u>unencumbered</u> (or ungrounded) by the dangers and pitfalls recalled in the left-brain. Drumming up alternatives or images is the **Conciliator's** strength. Just don't get this confused with *creating from nothing.* The **Conceptor** gives a *whole picture* in the future —

logic and all. The **Conciliator** gives a path — several — to *get* to the future.

Looking at these differences and becoming aware of how we judge them based on our *own brainstyle* is the basic truth of *The BrainStyles System™*. Once you figure out how you are judging others' intelligence and open yourself to the idea that you are looking at their *timing* in using their natural strengths, you'll be working alongside the most sophisticated of psychologists and brain researchers who are predicting "multiple intelligences."[1]

Risk Taking

Earlier in this book we defined taking a risk as taking a stand in the face of loss, or carrying forward a decision that has possible consequences of loss for the risk-taker's business and professional standing. When we talk about risk, we are talking about *considered* risk, risk taken in the context of the big picture. No person in any brainstyle considers what they're doing as "risky" at the time they are doing it. They see a problem to which they are applying their strengths.

The **Conciliator** operates best from feelings and acts impulsively — behavior which may look to others like risk-taking in its purest form. In fact, the **Conciliator** tends to *ignore* left-brain risk and consequences in the short term and, after thinking about it, to look for support and a fall-back decision for the long term.

Case in point: Mike became a pilot in the Marines because of the sheer challenges involved. As he puts it, "Where else at age 23 could I be responsible for millions of dollars' worth of equipment, and have as much fun?" What he enjoyed was testing himself to the limits. The "high" was getting back to the bar with all the other pilots, and being the star who had overcome all that (left-brain) technology with sheer (right-brain) guts.

"Sure, there was all the macho stuff — who could wear the darkest sun glasses, drink the most, fly the best. But competition wasn't the whole story, although I was in there to excel. The *real* game was to see how far you could go and not get 'caught' — push the edge of the envelope and invent the whole game on the way. Flying upside down under a bridge was not scary for me, although other pilots said it was stupid. For me, it was something I knew I had the skill and the problem-solving ability to do — no matter what came up in the middle of doing it." "Risk" was not the issue to Mike. The emotional high of testing intuition and reactions against the laws of gravity was all that counted. **Right-brain impulse + left-brain skill = quick, skillful, reactions without regard for consequences.**

The **Conciliator** will take interpersonal risks often. The **Conciliator** on a roll can be outspoken and beyond decorum. He can stride into any superior's office and demand an answer. He will confront leadership in ways that will leave his co-workers trembling. He is working from strength: knowledge of relationships; conviction and passion about values or goals.

Yet what the **Conciliator** is doing and what constitutes real risk are two different things. The **Conciliator** *does not consider the consequences of his actions until later.* In fact, what you get at **Time Zero** are emotional fireworks — not considered action. Consideration belongs to the left brain, and when the **Conciliator** acts at **Time Zero,** the left brain has not yet joined the process. Given some time, the **Conciliator** becomes aware of consequences, can pull back, change his mind, or regroup for an effective presentation, or longer-term commitments.

Being The Conciliator

Being a **Conciliator** is not easy, especially once your abilities and ambition carry you into management.

• Accept your feelings and how they let you work well with others. Call a *time out* if you get overwhelmed. Everyone will appreciate it. But <u>don't</u> spend time telling yourself to "stop being so emotional!" as so many in this brainstyle do. This is a futile mandate and will frustrate your efforts to use your feelings to contribute to others.

• Consider that your empathy for others may make you a

natural spokesperson for unstated concerns/ hidden agendas. Watch out for the trap of rescuing others who know you'll sympathize. Use your passion for furthering the progress of the *whole* group — including the boss. A win-win spokesperson takes time for (left-brain) preparation.

• Accept that other, left-brained styles are *faster* at *logic,* not "insensitive" or "uncaring." Watch for how you can *time* your influence.

• It may appear to you that those you manage will not live up to their commitments with the spirit you expect. Discuss goals. Look for heartfelt commitment only from *other* **Conciliators.** Use your natural ability to appreciate differences and to work with others as they are.

• Look for ways to use your great capacity to build coalitions and teams. You have the very best abilities to coach your team to turn in their best performances. Use other left-brainstyles to keep the focus on the time schedule, the priorities, and the plan. Your strengths aren't here, but you need minimal skill in these areas to bring in results.

• Look for assignments where the goals and aspirations are clearly articulated. Check your natural response to "do it yourself" or you might wind up doing it *all.* Use your natural gifts in communicating and negotiating to delegate.

• Ask for time to "sort the issue out" rather than simply resist the new idea or the direction. Ask what's possible.

• Understand that you do not have to be in touch with the future (be a visionary) because you *can find out who is* and take your lead from him. Your natural networking skills put you in touch with where the leading ideas are. Distinguish between coalition building and just plain socializing and gossiping by keeping your eye on the goal.

• When you know conflict is unavoidable (like giving a reprimand) rehearse the scene. Ask yourself, "What's the worst thing that can happen?" Then ask, "How can I handle that?" Anchor your emotions in a reasoned delivery.

• Watch out for projecting into the future based on one or two positive — or negative — events. Many **Conciliators** become alternately very ambitious then very depressed because a few events point to success or failure. Get input to define a longer view.

• Keep a journal, or take notes that you can review. Writing can help you get more objective as that right brain finds the words.

• Take time periodically to check that all your activity (all those lists) add up to your real purpose or top priority. You can lose the larger picture with all the distracting input you get from others and your attempts to respond to it all.

Chapter Six

The Deliberator

CHAPTER SIX

THE DELIBERATOR

de lib′ er ā tor: [a person who]
carefully weighs or considers
[who is] studied, intentional,
careful or slow in deciding.

At **Time Zero,** the **Deliberator** has a delayed, balanced response while he or she *assesses* a new situation. Unfamiliar information prompts a rapid search in the memory, where facts <u>and</u> feelings are stored. Many **Deliberators** have stored these as *standards* or the *right way to do things,* the rules for proceeding. The result is memory-based, or experienced, thinking and actions. Sometime afterward either right- or left-brain input is added so that many **Deliberators** can assess themselves at **Conciliators** or **Knowers.** The difference is that this brainstyle is more even-tempered over time and always has a **Time Zero** response that assesses while they rapidly recall. It does <u>not</u> mandate that the **Deliberator** brainstyle acts or thinks more slowly than other brainstyles.

According to our studies, we project the **Deliberator** to be the most numerous brainstyle in the population. Forty-eight percent of the target group observed are this brainstyle. Further, the authors commissioned a study by Professor Hurt of the University of North Texas' Department of Communications to test brainstyles. A majority of executives were found to be **Deliberators.**[1] These data support our contention that **Deliberators** are a majority of executives throughout corporate America.

Deliberators come in a wide variety of speeds and sizes, and, in our experience, are the most difficult to spot, precisely because of their strength for learning such a variety of information. (Comedians Johnny Carson and Lucille Ball are **Deliberators.**) They are the ones who can learn how to be quick at everything — once they have it mastered. So they can be *very rapid* (recalling, applying, synthesizing) at solving problems in their area of expertise. As one **Deliberator** put it who is naturally gifted at seeing the trees in the forest, "There's **Deliberators** in general, and then there's <u>me</u>." This statement really captures the precision that this brainstyle feels is the natural way of the world, and also the specific understanding for their own uniqueness that many in this brainstyle desire.

A visual representation of this brainstyle would look like this:

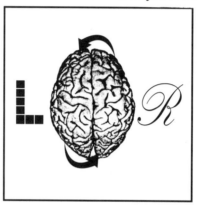

Put another way, the **Deliberator** does not respond at <u>**Time Zero.**</u> The stop might be no more than a pause, but the more unfamiliar the event, the longer it takes the brain to assess the information and assemble a response. "I don't just *react*" is a **Deliberator's** statement of pride about his or her thoughtful response.

Just because the **Deliberator** thinks before he speaks doesn't mean the response is necessarily slow in coming. An experienced **Deliberator** with memory banks packed with information on the subject can look just like a **Knower** — results-oriented, decisive, logical. But in an area where a person is comfortable with the subject, almost any brainstyle can look the same way.

The fact that the **Deliberator** works out of both the left and right sides of the brain means balance. It also means that there are learned behaviors in every area. The problem: **Deliberators** are most likely to be chameleons — trying to be all things to all people. Moreover, **Deliberators** can appear very different because they do so many things and at a wide variation in speed. The Renaissance men and women of industry who try for perfection in all things, they describe themselves as "results-oriented, factual, creative, people managers." Just ask them. As one very competent and competitive **Deliberator** reported after examining the details of brainstyles over a period of time: "I see myself performing in all of these brainstyle areas." He, and his **Deliberator** colleagues, often have the hardest time accepting the idea of *limits* to their strengths. (So do **Conciliators,** but for different reasons.) And they are the most likely to be confused (and confusing) about who they really are. **Deliberators** make a lot of promises about what they can deliver because of their abilities. **Time Zero** sorts out the real strengths of this brainstyle from the others and gives them a base of operations.

At 33, Greg had been on the fast track of a major oil company for several years. He was the hardest-working, most thorough and intelligent of his group. No problem was too complex or too technical. Greg challenged ideas, raced for the bottom line and usually was right when he got there. When asked about his strengths, his list was full of results. When brainstyles were explained to him, his response was quick: "I'm a **Knower.** I go for the bottom line — faster than anybody I work with." But after more information, Greg admitted that he prided himself on thinking before he spoke, on assessing ideas carefully before taking such rapid action. And so, as he started his own business a few years later, he sold himself very credibly to investors as someone who *analyzed* projects and *worked* conservatively *with high standards* rather than as an efficiency expert or someone with the strengths of a **Knower.** To get to that conclusion, Greg said he had to give up an image of himself he'd been very proud of for "one that is more true to me — who I really am. But I really can be fast on things I know about," he added.

Decision Making

At **Time Zero** the **Deliberator** cannot make a spontaneous decision. Complete decisions always require left/right brain activity, and until the **Deliberator** has reached into his memory to retrieve the necessary information, nothing happens. What confuses the issue is that sometimes the search takes place in a flash. Depending on previous learning, rehearsal or experiences that have been stored in memory, the **Deliberator** can *act like* a **Knower** or feel like a **Conceptor** — and sometimes even like a **Conciliator**. Spontaneous *expressions* of emotion are much less frequent for the **Deliberator** even though many report that they are aware of their feelings immediately in many situations. What is critical to know about the **Deliberator** is that *learning* — collecting, storing and retrieving information — *is the strength of this brainstyle.* This is why **Deliberators** are the most difficult to pin down at times, can have the most versatile behaviors, and *see themselves as a variety of strengths.*

For the **Deliberator,** a good decision is one that evolves naturally from what is already known. And, in many ways, the decisions of the **Deliberator** (once they get made) seem the wisest because they emerge from the prevailing wisdom. They validate past decisions by taking them as points of reference. The **Deliberator's** decisions are anchored, grounded. While the **Conceptor** looks out to the future for something that has no roots in the past (or that denies the rules of the present), the **Deliberator** seeks a base line from which to move in an orderly fashion. The aim of the **Deliberator** is to understand the rules, master the skills, and then play *better* (not faster) than anyone else.

Case in point: The December 1989 issue of *Inc.* profiled Steve Bostic, an "enterprising individual" who has plans for making his automated photo machine (bring in your negative and enlarge it yourself) a billion-dollar business in five years. Just as Steven Jobs, Ted Turner, and Trammell Crow define the **Conceptor** approach to business, Bostic is an eloquent articulator of the **Deliberator** point of view. In the cover interview, "Thriving On Order," Bostic explained his views on business planning and decision making related to business growth:

> I don't agree that growth has to be chaotic. I think that's a total myth. There may be chaotic moments and times of crisis, but it's completely unnecessary to deal from crisis to crisis. In fact that way of managing undermines your ability to grow.
>
> If you want to achieve significant growth, you need order, not chaos. You need to have things well planned and well thought out. Everybody has to be singing from the same hymn book.
>
> You have to take your vision, think it through, and turn it into consistent strategy. And then you have to get it on paper. That's key. I maintain that if you can't put your vision on paper, you can never do it in the real world.[2]

There can be very little question left concerning why the **Deliberator** Steve Bostic, who denies the existence of anything that isn't written down, and the **Conceptor** Tom Peters, who wrote *Thriving on Chaos*[3], have opposite views on the proper way to run a business. *Each is teaching his own brainstyle.* Neither one is right or wrong. Both are practical depending on who is running the company. The outcomes will be vastly different, of course.

Bostic's strengths are assessing, organizing, planning and improving, hence his photo machine business based on orderly decision-making. **Time Zero** events ("chaos") are kept to a minimum. He is *not* inventing new products or making technological breakthroughs. These are not his strengths. He gets his business to respond consistently. He applies his strengths to both the product delivered and the system used to deliver it.

It is the *fit* that produces the success for a brainstyle.

The strengths of the **Deliberator** are to assess, organize, and execute, not to decide and set priorities for new projects. For the inexperienced **Deliberator,** decision-making can be a fragmented, painstaking process. This can create a great deal of pressure for everyone — himself included. Getting the data, sorting it out, and testing for problems until the system is refined takes a long time. **Deliberators** can easily become undisciplined workaholics. They can generate lots of extra information/paper/meetings and cost a lot of overhead while they learn the best way to get to the goal. Subordinates in other brainstyles can decide that they are overworked and under-appreciated as they feed the data beast, who can never get enough. Unless there can be some productive conversations about how to use brainstyle timing, deadlines can be lost along with productivity and morale.

BrainStyle Clue:

*When called on to make a **Time Zero** decision, a **Deliberator** must first go to his memory to find a point of reference. You can jump-start the decision-making process by providing that point yourself: "This situation is similar to X ." "Here are 2 alternatives to choose from. Think about them and I'll get back to you by ____."*

But once **Deliberators** make a decision, watch out. From middle managers to chairmen to whole countries like Japan, **Deliberators** who have chosen a direction, a goal, and a solution to get there are awesome in their single-minded execution of a plan. Take Robert Swanson, founder of the bio-tech firm Genentech. When studied by Michael Meyer[4], he is described in the following way (and compared to Ross Perot, Steve Jobs, Ted Turner and other captains of industry):

> Swanson is formidable. He's the archetypal entrepreneur, a genuine pioneer. Of all the men in this book, only he deliberately and explicitly set out from the beginning to build an industrial empire. Not from

the time he found that his new venture would survive and prosper, mind you, but from the very first moment. The goal, Swanson said from day one, more than a decade ago, was to 'build Genentech into a one-billion dollar pharmaceutical company by 1990.'[5]

As Meyer adds, Swanson may be ahead of schedule.

A group of middle managers made up of **Deliberators** as the core team members, tackled a very complex operational problem. Fifteen months later, they declared objectives were reached amidst many distractions. The method? A step-by-step plan of *assess and test* with goals constantly measured and fed back to improve the process. And, as an aid, brainstyles were used: a **Knower** was brought into **Deliberator**-run meetings to facilitate the group in keeping a focus on the goals and to break up deadlocked decisions.

Conflict

The **Deliberator** prefers reason to fighting. And reason generally serves her well.

Every bit of logical and emotional information that a **Deliberator** encounters gets stored in a seemingly balanced "filing" system, going through both the right and left brain before storing. And so when the **Deliberator** reaches into memory, the recollection comes back in balance — the way it was filed. For the **Deliberator**, there are few, if any sudden surges of overwhelming emotions without some reason for them. Where there are no imbalances, there is evenness. Equilibrium represents a steady state: perfect balance on the highwire of life.

Ann served a term as President of a major Dallas charitable foundation for a year. As with most volunteer organizations, there were many sub-groups with different agendas and positions already in place as Ann took over leadership. Ann found she had a great deal of success directly linked to the application of her strengths:

- she prepared well in advance.
- she focused on a specific fund-raising goal.

- she defined objectives in key team areas.
- she met individually with each Board member and established mutual interests.
- she dealt with conflict indirectly, over time, by facilitating several discussions until a consensus was reached.

"I know we took longer," Ann assessed, "but I was comfortable leading this way. We reached our goals with everybody on board — and that was very important to me."

As a result of her left-brain/right-brain balance, the **Deliberator** is most comfortable when engaged in activity directed at making the world a rational, explainable place where there is — by definition — no conflict. The **Deliberator** sees shades of grey in almost everything. Where the world of the **Knower** is definitive, to the **Deliberator** it is a world of exceptions and specifics with no clear-cut answers. There *is* discussion. There *is* explanation. And there *must* be time to reflect before acting when the facts aren't in.

When faced with a conflict or a hurry-up situation, the **Deliberator** may get tense but not mad. This disinclination to get hot and bothered does not mean that a **Deliberator** will walk away from a fight. President Bush (a **Deliberator**) invaded Panama and Kuwait. He presented the first invasion as a planned, clearly articulated, *Four-Point Program.* We heard the reasoning and understood the logic. In contrast, President Reagan, the **Conceptor,** responded with more "passion." The invasion of Grenada and the target-bombing of Libyan "military installations" were simple, right-wrong, patriotic stands by Americans. We felt it. We were part of a cause. The logic was included in the concepts for the **Conceptor.** Comfort level on the part of the public can be linked to comfort with the method of decision-making.

Brainstyle dictates the way we fight. A **Deliberator,** in particular, tries to defuse conflict by explaining, discussing, and reviewing. But he will fight for what he thinks is *right.*

Every brainstyle picks its fights. The context varies with the personal strengths. Each brainstyle looks for opportunities to use its natural abilities — and, by extension, protect them. The

Deliberator is best at assessing, and in order to assess you need a set of standards. The **Deliberator** will fight for those standards or what is "right." His forays won't look like the emotional bombs of the **Conciliator,** but as a **Deliberator** must have said when his or her standards were violated, "Don't get mad, get even."

If the **Deliberator** does not like conflict, how then can people in this brainstyle be so fiercely competitive? Because they really do like to win. And it is in the race to be the best that they will, if necessary, pick their fights. The **Deliberators** compete by *mastering the game.* They therefore like to define the rules. Those who would change or override those rules are in for trouble. This is the standard movie plot starring **Deliberator** heroes like Clint Eastwood, Chuck Norris, or Charles Bronson. In real life as well, **Deliberators** are the calm, rational experts who have mastered the game just a bit better than the bad guys. Consultant gunslingers are hired for technical expertise to "trouble-shoot" and get us back on track — point out the "gaps," show us the plan, explain it all with a model.

Nobody learns the rules better than the **Deliberator,** and no one is better at playing hard and staying in bounds. Emotional conflict is out of bounds — but a hard-hitting debate to prove who is right — according to the rules — is appropriate for the **Deliberator.**

A problem: unlike the rules of grammar or tennis, which change once a millennium, business negotiations are quicksilver. "Rules" can apply in different ways on different days where people are involved. Now you see them, now you don't. What's more, other brainstyles — especially the **Conceptor** — play by their own rules. There is no universal standard — a fact that drives the **Deliberator** nuts. How is it possible to fight to win — to compete — without clear rules?

The **Deliberator** is at a loss in a situation with constant **Time Zeros:** Too much flexibility is required. And this is a non-strength of the brainstyle. *Brainstyle strengths which don't fit the situation cannot produce maximum results.*

A comparison of three **Deliberators** shows the importance of stored experience in producing competent actions and decisions: George Bush, Jimmy Carter, and Michael Dukakis each held government office. Bush, whose career involved jobs in all aspects of government, has had a much broader base to work from than the two former governors. They all approach decisions in a rational, analytical fashion. Carter, the nuclear engineer, is the man conceded to be the most "intelligent" but criticized for not being able to form his specific solutions into broad policies. Of the three, it is Bush who has the fewest **Time Zero** decisions at the level of complexity that the office of President offers. His actions and results in comparison with the other two of the same brainstyle are judged as more comprehensive and experienced. Experience counts for everyone, and especially for this brainstyle. Ask another experienced **Deliberator,** Henry Kissinger.

It is the **Deliberator's** great sense of orderly competitiveness that drives him up through the ranks to the top of the organization. As the **Deliberator** rises in the corporate structure, conflict is inevitable. Not all people want to be reasonable — or fit into the systems constructed to prevent problems. Knowing his strengths, the **Deliberator** can use other brainstyles as resources to prepare to respond to "unreasonable" conflict — to minimize the number of **Time Zeros.** Or, as the **Deliberator** nation Japan has taught us, *use time as the ally.* Stay with it until all the conflicts are aired and a consensus is reached. Certainly the **Deliberator** has the strengths to do this.

Conflict tends to smash the rules. Therefore the **Deliberator** will seek to maintain control by applying brainstyle strengths: organizing, preparing, applying structure to the situation.

BrainStyle Clue:

*Conflict resolution requires **Time Zero** decisions. **Deliberators** must expect this and use time accordingly: prepare ahead for the issues, build in time to think, prepare the other for a rational, delayed — not emotional — response.*

When the CEO does not surface and confront conflict issues directly, the effects on a company can be disastrous. It takes an unusual **Deliberator** CEO to face a problem directly. This looks too much like confrontation. It is more likely that she or he will try to prevent problems or circumvent them in a variety of ways. This takes time and resources. But once the problem has been addressed, the **Deliberator** has a chance to play to his strengths. He *can* take the role of mediator. He <u>can</u> plan a problem-solving session. He <u>can</u> set standards for resolution. The **Deliberator** *can* listen.

Case in point: Four years ago Fred was brought in as CEO for a recently deregulated utility company. He was charged with restructuring the company to be competitive and profitable in the 1990s. But senior management has yet to commit to the new policies and programs. There is much foot-dragging.

One problem seems to be that, along with his job, Fred inherited a senior management of veteran officers with an average tenure of twelve years. All thirty decline to openly voice opinions. They wait for the new boss to tip his hand, and then they agree — publicly. But there is only minimal follow-through on most of Fred's policy decisions.

Why are heads not rolling? Why are there not closed-door confrontations and "feet held to the fire" when policy subversion takes place right under Fred's nose? Because these are not his strengths.

Fred's strategy is a slow and steady, daily move toward changing the culture. He is examining the lowest ranks of management to prove his policies are necessary. In his view he is tackling issues and items *one by one* to build a case for his "strategy of the '90s" that will gradually erode the old way of doing things.

Confrontation is a natural non-strength of the **Deliberator.**

The '90s may be well underway before Fred finds that the conflict he wants to reason away is keeping business results from the bottom line in the time frame in which he has promised to deliver.

In contrast, another **Deliberator** chairman, Bob Crandall of American Airlines, uses the same strength of detailed analysis to "obsessively" go after details in a way that looks, sounds, and feels a lot like confrontation — at least as <u>Fortune</u> describes him as one "America's Toughest Bosses." **Deliberators** can look and sound very different. Toughness is energy focused in pursuit of a goal with more (or less) direct, left-brained evaluations thrown in. Crandall's perception is that he is pursuing facts, not confronting people. "His willingness to scrutinize the tiniest details, plus the encyclopedic knowledge he has acquired from that scrutiny, puts extraordinary pressure on executives to do likewise." Crandall is reported to use "an intimidating mixture of energy, verbosity, profanity, and bluff," reports <u>Fortune</u>[6]. And he gets results — people who focus on detail to execute a highly complex system very successfully.

BrainStyle Clue:

*The **Deliberator** responds to conflict or resistance with reason as a first choice.*
It takes time to resolve problems this way.

Learning

Teachers, especially those in public elementary schools, can only dream about classrooms filled with happy **Deliberators** waiting to read, absorb, analyze, and retrieve. No **Conciliator** personalizing, **Conceptor** disruptiveness, or **Knower** stubbornness. **Deliberators** are so receptive and, well, reasonable. American public school education was modeled on orderly progression: first grade, learn how to print; second grade, perfect printing; third grade, learn script. The **Deliberator** likes this sort of predictability; this brainstyle has an extremely high tolerance for the logic of the line.

Unlike the **Knower** and **Conciliator,** who store information in logical or emotional chunks, or the **Conceptor,** who stores atomic "thought-balls," the **Deliberator** stores in order. The **Deliberator** balances information and files (stores) it the same way. This means that **Deliberators** remember (retrieve) things the same way: in a balanced, rational way. At a **Time Zero** event, the other brainstyles can come up with an immediate response. The **Deliberator** comes up with questions, or, even better, the information read the night or week before.

For the **Deliberator,** knowledge is power. Therefore knowledge precedes action. They set up companies and institutions based on this value for knowledge.

The **Deliberator** looks to outside sources for knowledge. The working environment is critical to this brainstyle as a source of input. There is great importance placed on who they work with and whether they admire or respect their opinions.

The **Deliberator** values expertise. Evaluations of himself and others are based on how much is known on a subject (the quantity of data stored and able to be recalled), and whether the values are similar (a match of standards). Two **Deliberator** managers separately agreed that prior to learning about brainstyles, when they didn't approve of another's values, each would "write the guy off — just ignore him." After studying differences both concluded that they could appreciate the other guy's strengths and work with him very well — and leave the personal values to another time. Both also admit they struggle accepting **Conciliators** who react quickly — "too quickly, without the facts, as far as I'm concerned" — rather than thinking it over. Both are now looking for expertise from the **Conciliator** *after* the initial reaction.

Deliberators create cultures in which the ability to provide information — the right answer — is a major criterion for success, a culture in which knowledge of the rules and standards is critical to survival. School systems, highly technical companies, specialized firms of experts like attorneys or CPA's, and government agencies are examples of **Deliberator** cultures. Depending on the values, the brainstyle can measure and evaluate so relentlessly, the competition fostered can be ruthless, and status the prime goal. And so we have the competition of many school faculties measuring the students, then competing with one another for honors. On the other hand, many **Deliberator** companies, like Proctor & Gamble, have built on a strong value for people. Incorporating people into their methodical process to bring new products to market has meant a very caring environment for the individual.

Risk Taking

Of all the brainstyles, the **Deliberator** is least inclined to take risks — despite what other people may think he is doing. Risk taking requires an unusual amount of optimism about future prospects, and when anticipating the future the **Deliberator** is too aware of all the things that can go wrong. If the **Deliberator** cannot identify and neutralize risk in a new situation, forget it. He will not give it a GO.

Taking a risk requires making a decision now about something that may happen in the future. If the **Deliberator** hasn't heard of a similar situation working previously, he will not take the risk. If the situation is completely new to him, he will need lots of time to collect information and think it all through.

A **Deliberator** will avoid "placing at risk" more than he can afford to lose. And so, while he might invest discretionary funds in a high-risk, high-gain business opportunity, he will not do so very often, nor will he be likely to play fast and loose with his house, the kid's college money, or his pension fund. (This is not to say that those **Deliberators** who are experienced in the investment field cannot conclude that they alone can assess risk and overcome it with <u>your</u> money. For most, the *natural* response of this brainstyle is to assess and be cautious.)

However, what may look like a risk to others — trekking in the Himalayas, or leaving a powerful corporation to become an independent consultant — may be one the **Deliberator** has determined falls within the range of his capabilities and for which he will enjoy planning, then this brainstyle sallies forth with no thought of risk at all. The only real risk here is that the **Deliberator** may have miscalculated.

> *BrainStyle Clue:*
>
> *If you want to coax a **Deliberator** into taking a calculated risk, compare it to something that the **Deliberator** is familiar with and which has proven successful. Plan with him how to keep him in control.*

Risk, even calculated risk, denies the risker direct control over the outcome. The **Deliberator** hates to give up control.

Managing The Deliberator

To manage the **Deliberator** effectively, you must be aware of the fact that he wants to be everything and do it all — personally. So it is very difficult to keep people in this brainstyle from simultaneously signing up for karate lessons, singing lessons, and language lessons even if they have only slight aptitudes in these areas. A **Deliberator** with good physical coordination and above-average intelligence is especially vulnerable to being trapped in a tangle of conflicting interests and expectations for himself. He has received so much respect and encouragement from all the teachers along the way who have admired his ability to memorize and retrieve information that he spends whole careers overcommitting himself and his organization at the expense of his family and personal life. *Balance is lost when the **Deliberator** believes the outside (behavior) instead of the inside (brainstyle).*

Case in point: Tom, a financial manager, appears assertive, yet warm and charming. He looks his interviewer directly in the eye when explaining how excited he is about his work. People have told him he is one of the best at his job — a "real leader." He is articulate and describes business situations brilliantly and thoroughly.

He describes his strengths as "being bright, flexible, a good people person, able to spot a good business deal, bottom-line-oriented, and highly ethical." In fact, he finds the idea of having only one set of strengths limiting. *This is not what he's been told.* He believes he is good at most things, or could learn them if he didn't know them already.

He says, "A particular strength of mine is an ability to appear as the other person wants me to appear. I'm a *chameleon.*"

In further discussion with Tom, he agrees that he considers alternatives and others' input only on deals or in business areas where he has had experience. No, he does not do this with new projects. He must study those.

It is a paradox that the **Deliberator** is most productive, effective, resourceful, and competitive when his boundaries are most closely defined. Give people in this brainstyle sidelines and a goal and you literally set them free.

Tom is trying to get investors to set him up in a firm that screens and funds small businesses. He fails to get backers because, he is told, he has too little focus and wants 70% control. He took a position inside a firm as an investment banker and successfully executed a number of projects.

BrainStyle Clue:

Once any project has been roughed out, put the ***Deliberator*** *in charge of shaping it up. He will tighten what needs to be tightened and loosen what needs to be loose according to the standard.*

Warning: The ***Deliberator*** *can be a perfectionist and tinker with last details beyond the value they add to the project. Unless you say halt, he can and will refine until or beyond the deadline.*

Here are some other keys to the **Deliberator** brainstyle that will help you find the right "fit" for him or her.

• A **Deliberator** cannot make fast decisions in new areas. If you push him, you will only make him tense — you may get a "Yes," but you won't get the real decision you want.

• This brainstyle does not respond emotionally. Do not assume that a lack of enthusiasm means a lack of interest. **Deliberators** are excited on the inside. They are naturally suspicious of other brainstyles who show their feelings on the outside — unless they know about brainstyles.

• In some cases, a **Deliberator** can look spontaneous <u>and</u> intuitive or responsive early on. (This is why many **Deliberators** think they are **Conciliators**.) Barry, a venture capitalist, explained that he was able to free up his assessment of a project to consider alternatives, to go with his "gut feel," soon after realizing he was experienced in an area. He said, "<u>**Time Zero**</u> clarified for me that I assess the facts or feelings *first* — then very quickly am aware of my intuition. I always thought before that I was an 'intuitive banker.' I don't compare to a **Conciliator,** though. I'm more reasonable. And I use my intuition second — after I get the facts."

• **Deliberators** can look like other brainstyles <u>after</u> **Time Zero**. The test to determine brainstyle is what comes first and is the real basis for comfort.

• A **Deliberator** does not delegate well. His gift at refining and improving requires that he have all the information in front of him at the same time. Ask the **Deliberator** to set up plans and systems to achieve goals *with* his people. A planned approach works best.

• A **Deliberator** will volunteer to do any job that sounds interesting to him. Do not confuse genuine interest with competence.

Working for the Deliberator

If you can determine that you are working for a **Deliberator,** here are some tips for dealing with a brainstyle that is sometimes seen as being aloof or unresponsive:

• The **Deliberator** shows how. He doesn't show off.

• The **Deliberator** states the criteria for success, and then leads by example. He wants others to do their part because it's the right thing to do.

• The **Deliberator** leads others by explanation. *The assumption of every brainstyle is that everyone operates the same way.* The **Deliberator** assumes that once you understand why, you are motivated. Subordinates are implementors directed by the system or the plan for the **Deliberator.** Do not expect to get broad overviews or pep talks. Use this person for what she or he can deliver.

• Subordinates who can prove their ideas, who are not "flashy," and who support their boss by preventing surprises are the most comfortable for this brainstyle. When this is not you, you need to negotiate. Jamal, a young **Conceptor,** chose banking as a career. After being fired from one job as a loan officer for a whole series of personal offenses — "I was too flashy" — Jamal decided to market his strengths to the **Deliberator** banker culture. "I can talk the language of our customers," Jamal said in his next job interview. "I'm the kind of guy these commercial real estate deal makers can relate to. I can be a translator — a middle man between them and the bank." Jamal was hired with the understanding he was "different from the average banker" and with much greater success and longer tenure.

• If a **Deliberator** has a problem with something you are doing, do not expect him to deal with it directly. Instead, he may just act unhappy or ask questions. If you ask, he will give you a reasoned explanation of why his way is right and yours isn't. The **Knower** would have confronted you. The **Deliberator** will not — but listen carefully anyhow. He will prefer to negotiate differences, step by step.

• If you are assigned a project by a **Deliberator,** follow directions and bring back what you were asked to bring, along with another alternative you may like better. Show what the pitfalls are in each. Influence the project with information about how to prevent problems. The **Deliberator** may want to do the deciding himself. Don't push a decision, ask for another meeting. You'll need to do your homework to get a vote. And stay with it. Perseverance is the strength of this brainstyle. They listen to it in others.

• If you get stuck on a project, go to the **Deliberator** for a re-assessment of the problem. Don't get hung up on what may sound "negative," **Deliberators** are best at determining the *gap* between where we are and where we should be. Being helpful and informative is what the **Deliberator** does well. Often this comes out as critique. Use the input to strengthen your execution of the plan.

• The **Deliberator** who works hard to get things right will expect you to do the same if you don't discuss strengths. **Conceptors** and **Conciliators** must set up realistic expectations with a **Deliberator** when working in their non-strength regarding attention to detail, otherwise the session can degenerate into nit-picking or worse — a judgment of these two brainstyles as incompetent in <u>everything</u> based on their non-strength with details.

Being The Deliberator

Being a **Deliberator** becomes uncomfortable only when there is a bad "fit" — the match between your strengths and the demands of the job. Until that time, you are the one who gets rewarded for your reports, your innovations, your professional calm. There may be a few who grouse about your "people skills," but you are diplomatic enough and friendly enough to get over these hurdles.

• You value reason and the harmony reason brings. The bad surprise is that the higher you go, the more people seem to lose their senses. Rationality does not prevail, and you are asked to make fast decisions without the necessary information. You are also asked to install solutions with more people involved — more stakeholders.

• Your strength is in organizing, improving, and refining. Seek out others who will work with you on defining the Big Picture. Include those who can address people and communication issues.

• Set up systems that will allow you to deal with information in the *time frame you need* to make timely decisions. This means *pre*-planning, *previewing*, *before* well-structured meetings kick off with *clearly defined goals.*

• Alert those who work above and below you (especially the

Knowers in your life) that your responses to requests for decisions may not be quick, but they will be thorough and carefully considered.

• Those in other brainstyles want some responses from you, e.g., "Good Morning," "I'm trying to understand how you feel," "I'll get back to you in an hour with a next step" to keep informed about you because you don't show how you feel as much as they may show feelings. Bulletins help.

• Don't make the mistake that the **Deliberator** Gary Hart made: People do <u>not</u> separate your ideas from your actions. You will be expected to implement the ideas others think you are committed to. Clarify what you are committing to and what you are not.

BrainStyle Application Section

A BRAINSTYLE APPLICATION

"Weaknesses" vs. Non-Strengths vs. Self-Criticism

Most of us do not know how to communicate with the language of strengths. What follows is a section to get you started. When someone describes something about you as a "weakness," they do so because of their own expectations. They undoubtedly want you to do something well that they do well and you do not. When you try to live up to *others'* expectations rather than negotiate relationships based on your *natural* gifts, you lose — in self esteem, and effectiveness — and so do they.

When you are acting fully in your strength, you are most *unlike* anybody else in any other brainstyle. You *are full of yourself,* and others may find that fullness unlike the way *they* do things. Conventional wisdom says: "Strengths taken to extremes are weaknesses. Modify your behavior. Pull back." We say, keep focusing on your strengths. The discipline to master strengths where you bring the most value will occur — naturally. You will not be competing or acting inappropriately. Win-lose competition happens most often when we try to excel in our non-strengths, and this often gets started when people tell us to change.

A "non-strength" can easily be defined as someone else's (another brainstyle's) strength. It is <u>not</u> what we tell ourselves it is when we're not good at something. For example, your strength may be that of the right-brained **Conciliator.** You are excellent at "personalizing" or making the job and issues personally meaningful. Your *non-strength* is <u>not</u> the fact that you "take things personally." This is your <u>strength</u>, adding feelings to data. It may be that you don't like this aspect of your strength. Others may get uncomfortable with your emotions. Or you may use your emotions as a reason to try to get others to change ("if you do that I'll be hurt"). These are all the complicated judgments we add on to the basic facts of our strengths. Your *non-strength as a* **Conciliator** *is collecting and receiving data in an objective, neutral way.* Your brainstyle does not do this with new information. Most people define their *non-strength* as a "weakness" like this: "I get <u>too</u> emotional about things. This is a weakness and something I'd like to change." This is the mistake. The brainstyle dictates the emotional response. It will be the acceptance of this fact that will allow you to express this gift as: "I react personally to information, so when someone gives me some feedback, I need time to react and think it over."

Now try the following exercise to help you change your judgments into the underlying brainstyle strengths and non-strengths.

A BrainStyle Exercise

Make a list in the "weakness" column of all your personal judgments. Use the brainstyle chapters to name the strengths underlying your judgment. Then go to the description of the brainstyle you may be comparing yourself to, and write in their strength.

Translating "Weaknesses" or Self-Judgments
Into Strengths and Non-Strengths

"Weakness"	Strength	Non-Strength
my judgment about me	natural ability	learned ability/ experience

Example:

1.	*too slow*	*methodical*	*responsive*
		thorough	*spontaneous*
2.			
3.			

Think about how you describe others. Try the same exercise with them:

	Gossip or Judgment about another	Underlying strength	Underlying non-strength
1.	*hysterical*	*responds with*	*neutral, dealing*
	reactive	*feeling first*	*from experience*
2.			
3.			

To use this exercise, look at ways to build on your strengths and use them as a resource for others. At the end of each of the four brainstyle chapters there are suggestions about how to do this. In the first example of a "weakness," "too slow" was given. This **Deliberator** can either focus on building areas of expertise where speed of recall will naturally increase, or, in new areas, set realistic expectations for speed. In either case, making it a negative to be methodical and thorough loses the power these strengths can add. Trying to be like a **Conciliator** — *responsive* or *spontaneous* — will have limited results, increased frustrations, and hold out the promise that you can be something you're not. Everyone loses by trying to play a phony game. As you continue in your descriptions of others, ask yourself: how can I start identifying their strengths instead of being distracted by their behaviors?

This is not a new process for you. You do it with your close friends all the time. You look past how they act at times because you know *who they really are.*

When you are most yourself and appreciate your own gifts, you create your own self-esteem and contribute more clearly. Otherwise you will believe it when others tell you to change so they will feel more comfortable. This is a neat way to make you responsible for their comfort.

Look in the "Self-Help" section of the bookstore. There you will find books, each teaching you how to act like its author, to improve by changing yourself into something else. YOU WILL IMPROVE YOURSELF BY BEING MORE YOURSELF.

PART III

TO KNOW THYSELF
IS TO LOVE THYSELF
<u>AND</u> THY NEIGHBOR

Chapter Seven

How BrainStyles Work Together:
There Are No Bad BrainStyles,
Only Bad Fits

How Each BrainStyle Is Seen By Others

When we are comfortable with another, we often describe them in this way:

Knower

When Comfortable
with the BrainStyle

Direct,
Straight-Forward,
Decisive,
Aggressive, or
Shrewd

Conceptor

When Comfortable
with the BrainStyle

Challenging,
Visionary,
Optimistic, Sees the
big picture,
Experimental,

Conciliator

When Comfortable
with the BrainStyle

Warm, Enthusiastic
Accepting, Supportive
Tactful, Imaginative
Spontaneous, or
Empathetic

Deliberator

When Comfortable
with the BrainStyle

Deliberate, Systematic
Neutral, Objective
Private, Thoughtful
Cautious, Methodical

But when the same person acts the same way and we are uncomfortable with what they do, we label it like this:

Knower

When Uncomfortable

Dictator, Bully,
Inflexible,
Insensitive to others
or unfeeling, Type "A"

Conceptor

When Uncomfortable

Manipulative,
Blue-sky, Unrealistic,
Controlling, of ideas with no
follow through on details

Conciliator

When Uncomfortable

Self-absorbed,
Defensive, Personalizes
everything, cannot take
feedback, an idealist,
Moody, Wishy-washy

Deliberator

When Uncomfortable

Rigid, Silent, Self-
interests are only agenda,
a loner, Paralyzed with
indecision, a perfectionist,
no priorities.

CHAPTER SEVEN

HOW BRAINSTYLES WORK TOGETHER: THERE ARE NO BAD BRAINSTYLES, ONLY BAD FITS

The essence of the high-performing system is good "fit," not the rigid culture that requires everyone to "fit in." Respect for the individual strengths of the different members of the team can produce excellence. The culture that commands conformity or comfortability breeds "politics" in the worst sense — where what you say matters far more than what you contribute.

A competent CEO uses conflict to further the business. A company built on strengths mean that "personality conflicts" vanish because everyone's brainstyle "fits" his job. Ensuring that people are respected for their strengths rather than for their ability to make people comfortable is an essential value to ensure high performance.

Let us examine, then, the ways in which each of the four brainstyles performs in combination with the others.

The Knower at Work

When the rapid left-brain **Knower** is working on an idea, he is probably the only person who is aware that the "percolating" process is going on. He does his best thinking alone, and in control. He literally does not have a need to share information. He is quite sure that nobody else will understand what he is doing and that they will just mess up the thinking process with illogical input or disagreements if he does share with them.

Unlike the **Conciliator,** who gathers data by conferring with as many people as possible, the **Knower** uses unilateral methods, such as reading or interviewing. Moreover, in a **Knower** *interview* (as opposed to a **Conciliator** *discussion*) the point is to gather information, not to let others in on the plan — until it's 80% shaped and solid.

Once a **Knower** lets one of his ideas into the light, you can be sure that the idea is primarily up for ratification, not discussion. Only an equally strong response will cause the **KNOWER** to pause.

BrainStyle Clue:

As a manager, the **Knower** *thinks about the task at hand before the needs of the people involved in completing them. The* **Knower** *will tend to keep final control and assign out only the work and not the decisions.*
Most **Knowers** *will do best in charge of managing systems or crises that require decisive, short-term action.*

To make good use of the **Knower's** gifts, you must make sure there is a specific job fit. A position that requires quick logic and structure at **Time Zero,** like getting things started, coming up with new and focused goals or projects, keeping a job on schedule, developing a strategy, and persuading with logic are suited to the **Knower** applicant. There will be problems for the **Knower** if the job description calls for someone with *right-brain* qualities — relationship skills, like sales, or blue sky thinking, strong team or diplomatic skills.

Case in point: Tim owns a company that specializes in setting up new office buildings with office furniture. Once the plans have been made and all the furniture ordered, he brings in a team to set up the offices — one man to an office.

One **Knower** team leader for a set-up crew works at an incredible speed. Working alone, he is lightning. For getting the job 90 - 95 percent finished, this crew leader gets his crew to perform better than any other. But he always has a problem when the plan needs adjusting. Maybe the wrong chairs arrived. Maybe the client changes the room arrangement. Instantly the job requirement changes from <u>executing</u> the plan to modifying it and negotiating with people.

At this point, the speed wizard loses his edge. Focusing on his own goal, he moans, "This was not part of the plan!" He can't negotiate with other goals. He wants to reinstitute the plan. He is at a **Time Zero** event, and his right brain has no quick way to supply him with the flexibility to revise.

Imagine the potential for this man if he were given an assignment that fit his strengths. For instance, what if his job was *only* to handle the first 90 percent of the installations? If he could be in charge of the system every time, and then bring in the people-oriented, patient negotiators to finish up with the clients, everyone could win.

Bringing Out the Best

Managing **Knowers** isn't an easy job, but it can be done once you understand how his brain speed works. Play to **Knowers'** strengths by giving their gift of linear, logical thinking a chance to work. Here are some hints.

• **Knowers** can put together future plans that are easily understood, give clear direction, and combine ideas in new ways. They will not include the whole picture, however, and work well in concert with a **Conceptor.** Or **Conciliators** and **Deliberators** can round out the plan using their strengths.

• **Knowers** are best at sorting information to get to a result. They can be inventive at finding solutions to problems that get in the way. Use their planning abilities.

• **Knowers** make fast, logical decisions, so go to them <u>early</u> to influence their plans or goals. Give them alternative solutions or goals to choose from. Don't pose problems unless you want <u>their</u> answer. Once they have set a course, it is difficult to influence them to change.

• When you must argue with a **Knower**, challenge his conclusions. **Knowers** arrive at conclusions and then back them up with facts. The minute you start arguing details, you are going to the bottom of the "stack" (information filed in the brain) and trying to move the whole thing in a piece. Start with the big picture and let the other guy do the rearranging.

• **Knowers** have no ready access to right-brain feelings. Put the **Knower** in charge of managing systems first, then people. Make people-assignments part of the task of collecting information and following through.

• **Knowers** are excellent individual contributors. Delegate tasks to them that require swift, solo execution. Better yet, give them start-up or turn-around projects that require systems solutions.

• **Knowers** rarely take personal risks because risk is illogical. They do take control, and when in charge, do not see a project as risky. Put them in charge of executing plans for the future. They may hesitate when it comes to personally investing in the plans. Don't assume that *take charge* means *take the plunge.*

• Finally, the **Knower** may not be a good team player, but he makes an exceptionally good member of the team. Do not confuse the strength of his logic with self confidence. **Knowers** don't often ask, but do care deeply that they are on the right track — especially with people. Tell them when they are. You may have to add that this is part of the job.

Working for the **Knower** *can be tricky, especially if you are a* **Knower** *yourself.*

Once you know that your supervisor or any other manager is a **Knower**, you have the knowledge to position yourself from your own strengths. Here are some tips that will make your life with a **Knower** much easier.

• The **Knower** will be abrupt. It isn't personal. You can be very direct in return. Speak up.

• The **Knower** will require fast decisions. If you can't keep up, explain in bottom-line terms why you must perform differently or why you disagree. (as Gary did in Chapter One). **Knowers** can take in a great deal of information once they see how what you have to offer will get them to the goal. (It won't take long either.)

• The **Knower** really doesn't register how you *feel* about something early on. Don't present him with an idea until you have a grasp of the logic behind it. If you do give your feelings, put them in terms of how they will affect the result.

• The **Knower** will tend not to delegate authority on new projects. Don't expect it. Ask logical questions and learn. Negotiate for authority based on results.

• The **Knower** admires competence. If you share his agenda, you have a useful ally, or a very protective boss. It's often black or white, friend or foe. You certainly want a **Knower** on your side. To get him or her there, show that you can deliver results.

Finding The Fit

If you are a **Knower,** here are some tips for marketing yourself — and starting a constructive collaboration — to an uncomprehending business world.

• Don't claim to be a "team player." This is not your strength. Explain that you are most comfortable working alone or in charge of a piece of the work. With your cards on the table, you are ready to negotiate a real role for yourself as a team member.

• Position yourself as the one on the team who can see through the clutter, define the end result, and simplify the strategy in **Time Zero** situations. *However,* one answer, derived alone, is *not* the one that is going to get the most commitment. *Use your quick answer as a focus for the team, then get other input.*

• Exploit your individual contributions. Explain to others that as long as there is a system in place, you can work faster than anyone. But be sure to build in a way to get some help — or input — if the system derails or must be adjusted through negotiation.

• Add practicality to the dreams of the risk takers. And add it *after* those other very sensitive brainstyles are past their initial **Time Zero** offerings. This is when every brainstyle is the most vulnerable. Mature **Knowers** are able to use their experience and quick judgment to both visualize the future product as well as identify potential potholes as a way of getting to the desired result. Critiquing another's new idea for being impractical because you can see all the potential negatives must be carefully timed. Think of the other brainstyles as creating a possible arena for you to perform in. They need <u>you</u> to make their dreams work.

• Structure projects with pre-set reporting dates. People will bother you less if they know exactly when you will make your report.

• Acknowledge and <u>use</u> others' expertise in your areas of non-strengths: people, detail, follow-through, or concepts, for example. Being realistic about your non-strengths creates the basis for honest delegation.

• Make sure you understand *their* version of the goals before you spend your valuable time devising systems to achieve them.

• Explain over and over and over that what you are saying is not personal — it is your judgment. Your left brain delivers quick critiques and conclusions. More than anything, this interferes with others' *timing* in reaching their own conclusions. Allowing them a little time can make a difference.

• Remember, when people in other brainstyles frustrate you, it's because their brains work differently and at a different speed than yours. Figure out what brainstyle they are in. *The problem is time. The solution is time.* It will help others if you present your ideas and tell them how you are quick to make judgments (rapid left brain) yet still want the strengths they bring. You can work out a way to *time* your problem-solving instead of asking that either of you change.

• Your non-strength is listening for detail or listening empathically without quick interpretation. Develop a minimum of skill in listening to exactly what the other person is saying. Others speak often in terms you may not relate to. Help yourself focus and keep in communication with them in short meetings, by note-taking, paraphrasing, or whatever works for you. Most important is an honest statement that will help the other focus so you can better attend to them: "I'm not as good with the process or background as you are. If you start with the results first, I'll be able to track better and give you a better response." This is *not* the same as "Just cut to the chase."

The Conceptor at Work

How you feel about working for a **Conceptor** will depend largely on when in his career you encounter him. Early on, the **Conceptor** is likely to seem so egotistical and "off the wall" that unless you are enraptured by his vision (the Steve Jobs Effect) you cannot imagine working for someone so controlling. Besides, you may never be able to get a word in edgewise. This brainstyle often requires a forum to talk through ideas (as does the other right-brainstyle, the **Conciliator** — who makes friends to do so). Until the concepts begin to form, there is a great need to look at the whole picture — which can mean everybody in the room.

Here are some things to keep in mind.

• **Conceptors** need to develop focus through working on the nitty-gritty. By working in several areas early on and being pushed to look at a variety of specializations, their concepts will have more reality.

• **Conceptors** are excellent at direction and priority setting. They will contribute most at the front end of a project, looking out to define new directions and possibilities.

• **Conceptors** have trouble recognizing and appreciating the difficulties involved in execution and attention to detail important to other brainstyles. To get a **Conceptor's** attention, *timing* is critical in bringing these out. In the early stages of a project or new solution, questions or points about execution interfere with the creative process. The **Conceptor** wants to establish a GO/NO GO. It's broad brush at first. Later, after some basics of the overview are nailed down, these points are invaluable.

• A **Conceptor** can act like a **Knower** on one subject and a **Conciliator** on another. Don't expect evenness. Expect passionate ideas.

Just because **Conceptors** have vision when it comes to problem-solving doesn't mean life is a breeze when it comes to managing their own careers. Two women **Conceptors** (growing up in very different parts of the country) Karen (30) and Jean (39), discussed career choices they had made and how they had made them. Each was very good at both artistic as well as "hard" subjects like math and science. When it was time to go to college, both women wanted to study a more *right-brained* subject — art history in Karen's case, fashion and design in Jean's case. Each of the women's fathers counseled them to study a major that would earn money. Jean majored in business. Karen got an engineering degree. Each woman was successful early in complex jobs requiring broad analysis and design skills: creating a whole picture while also designing the details. Karen, while still in her twenties, earned a six-figure salary restructuring a major bank and all its organizational systems. Jean was promoted for addressing organizational issues as she installed newly designed computer systems.

Karen left her fast track position. Jean is about to. Their stories are similar: both are bored by purely left-brain applications: designing and assessing systems. They yearn for more holistic applications of their strengths. Karen wants to pursue a degree in architecture, Jean wants something in the fashion industry.

Their challenge in envisioning a future which applies their gifts is as difficult as anyone else's who is factoring in what they "should" do. Their strengths are the motivation to change and the reason for dissatisfaction: they each need a place with more balance between hard-edged analysis and creativity. Their horizons are large. Finding a fit on the way up has had to be made at the same pace they are becoming comfortable with their own strengths.

Bringing Out The Best
• **Conceptors** need other brainstyles to assess and implement their plans; yet they don't like spending time on the details nearly as much as on the ideas. Their impatience can easily be labeled "non-support" by others ("He has <u>no idea</u> of the work that went into this!"). This is simply a **Conceptor** non-strength showing up. You will have to make it <u>your</u> job to get the information to the **Conceptor** in a way that will be appreciated. Remember: *you will never be appreciated by another brainstyle the way you will by*

someone in your own brainstyle.

• Challenge change for change's sake with a **Conceptor.** If there are too many new ideas, confront the fact directly — no one can work on more than two or three top priorities and do them excellently. Present plans to make **Conceptor** ideas workable. Other brainstyles get things done. But don't let the **Conceptor** get out of touch with the project. That rapid left-right-brain processing must solve problems along the way and provide follow-through, even though it is not a strength to do so.

• In meetings **Conceptors** demand their own outline: big ideas first and skip the details. Under time pressure, they rush to the Big Picture. They show stress by demanding punchlines from others. Along the way there can be many **Time Zero** decisions. The demand for well-thought out, speedy decisions in the future stresses the **Conciliators** and **Deliberators.** These brainstyles need to be brought in when their buy-in is crucial to execution. This does not mean that everyone has to be at the same meeting all the time. Using brainstyle timing, several short meetings can be structured with sub-groups who prepare ahead.

Case in point: A team of Customer Service Managers were gathered by their **Conceptor** director from all over the country to formulate, for the first time, a set of national policies — rather than the regional ones they had previously been using. After a brainstyles workshop, the group decided that sub-grouping worked best for the **Deliberator/Conciliator** group. They would meet the night before their meeting with "the Chief," discuss and post ideas all over a hotel room until they reached agreement. The meetings in which decisions were to take place the following day began taking one-third the time and covered more topics, with everyone well prepared. The **Conceptor** boss was able to use his strengths to strategize, give overviews and even challenges that the team felt comfortable with *because they were not at* **Time Zero.** Prior to this, the meetings had been strained; there was a lot of "going along with what the boss wants" — the team was unable to make decisions at the pace of the **Conceptor** boss. Resentments were building and follow-through lagging.

• **Conceptors** can be very warm, personable, and forgiving with people and their personal problems. They are flexible and have the capacity to understand mistakes or changes in a way that other brainstyles can't. Pose solutions after taking responsibility for a mistake with a **Conceptor** and see if you cannot move ahead quickly.

Finding The Fit

Being a **Conceptor** is not an easy experience. You are very clear in your own mind that you have incredible insights and that you are better equipped than others to deal with the big problems that face you, others, or your company. You can see ahead faster than they can. The difficulty comes in telling them your ideas. Timing is critical. And patience.

• Knowing about brainstyles can help you understand that your gift is seeing an unknown future. You must enroll others in coming up with support, data, and ways to get there. You are a natural at people management — once you understand how the gifts of others can work with yours to achieve a mutually beneficial result. You have the passion and ideas.

• In order to avoid the frustrations of being the **Conceptor** in what appears to you to be an ignorant and slow world (the numbers of **Knowers** and **Conceptors** are fewer by far than of **Conciliators** and **Deliberators**), and in order to control and re-order the universe as you know it is supposed to be, remember this: You can always *get control over others by getting them to do what they are going to do naturally anyway.* Work on the goals. Save yourself from enormous frustration and be more in control of your own tremendous energy. When people are doing what they do best, they will not find your energetic encouragement either bossy or arrogant. *Simple.* (Okay, not *easy.*)

• Invest your best energies in your natural gift for creating visions — complete ones, not just ideas — for the future. You have the only left brain/right brain interaction that will allow a complete concept to shape up beyond the horizon. If people in your brainstyle don't do it, nobody else will — because they can't.

 • **Conciliators** are potentially the best audience when **Conceptors** are developing ideas. They can supply the imaginative support needed to take a concept from disjointed metaphors and images to a full-blown solution. Get an agreement *up front* with this other brainstyle about how you'll work together, or the imaginative **Conciliator** may continually compete for the lead, ("What about *my* ideas?" "Let's try this!") especially in creative discussions.

 • **Deliberators** are the best partners for objectively **assessing** an idea, a person, a project. They can cover your non-strengths in evaluating against criteria and planning execution.

 • **Knowers** are the best partners in formulating strategies that need hard-edge, straight line clarity. You probably already enjoy their company in planning.

 • To protect *yourself* from multi-project melt-down, set priorities in a few areas. Concentration helps you deliver what you say you will deliver.

 • Manage Your Non-Strengths. Keep your word — no matter how many irons you have in the bonfire and how old yesterday's projects may seem today. Follow-through is your non-strength. If you can't personally follow up on projects that have been set in motion, make sure there is somebody who will.

Managing The Conceptor

We may as well lay it on the line: the **Conceptors** are basically "unmanageable" in the traditional sense of the word. That is why in school and early in their careers they are considered insufferable egotists or unrepentant rule-breakers. Their right-brained colleagues, the **Conciliators,** are not far behind. The **Conciliators** just make more friends as they brag, rebel, and tell their stories. As students, those in this brainstyle think they know more than their teachers. (They may be only faster to see the issue.) As junior employees, they are likely to take liberties that only the VP's take as their due. They may be tossing out rules and creating policies to make new playing fields for possibilities. It is not *easy* to deal with this brainstyle.

• **Conceptors** *need* a team; yet they are *not* natural *team players*. The gift of the quick left/right brain response is that the one who possesses it has immediate whole ideas based on both feeling <u>and</u> logic. This tends to *exclude* others at first. The brainstyle needs to constantly collect acquaintances and engage them in conversation in order to detail and refine the concept. With the input, the **Conceptor** can invent a plan for putting the concept into action while exciting others about a new idea.

• **Conceptors** need the challenge of whole projects. Pieces drive them nuts and will not receive their best work.

• **Conceptors** may forget to stop and get involvement <u>or</u> commitments from those in brainstyles with a gift for follow-through. Because of their involvement with their *own* right-left brain exchange, they forget to acknowledge **Deliberator's** and **Conciliator's** contributions. They are caught up in their own thought processes. They can sound arrogant. They can get too involved with starting new projects of their own and let previous ones drop.

• **Conceptors** need to build minimal skills in non-strengths in order to manage others: systems, details, execution. They will *not* become as good at them as will other brainstyles, of course.

• **Conceptors** are at their best creating *new* answers. They are used most effectively at start-up or at trouble spots.

• **Conceptors** want personal recognition for achievements (although not as frequently as **Conciliators** do).

The Conciliator at Work

• When the **Conciliator** is at work on a new idea, everybody will know it because he openly solicits input. He does his best thinking with others, because his gift is coming up with imaginative options that need to be bounced back for logical, left-brain input.

• Unlike the **Knower,** who works unilaterally on the front end without need for consensus, the **Conciliator** works multilaterally in an attempt to build a whole plan with expertise from the right sources. On the way, a consensus can emerge. Other brainstyles can perceive this as socializing. Without a clear goal, it can be. It is also *networking*. Networking needs a focus. It is natural for the **Conciliator** brainstyle. It is also, according to research of the last seventeen years,[1] the "power tool for advancing up the career ladder."[2] The **Conciliator's** natural need for contacts and ability to make them has been recognized as a business asset:

> Only recently has networking been more broadly defined as a complex of knowledge, skills, and attitudes that lends itself to individual, group, and organizational effectiveness (McHale, 1987)... *networking* is defined as "the ability to create and maintain an effective, widely based system of resources that works to the mutual benefit of oneself and others."[3]

Other brainstyles network as well. When **Knowers** or **Deliberators** carry out what is defined as *networking* by Byrum-Robinson and Womeldorff[4], they do it differently, of course, because of a more left-brained, focused approach. These two brainstyles are more apt to seek out people who can assist on a specific task. They may or may not form friendships along the way as the **Conciliator** does.

• Once the **Conciliator** has brought influence to bear on a decision, and has discovered agreement, he can move rapidly and impatiently toward a conclusion. **Conciliators** can be very pushy and demanding once committed. All the feelings are driving for a resolution. This is why many in this brainstyle think they are **Knowers.**

• If the **Conciliator's** conclusions are challenged, he immediately incorporates the other points of view — thus neutralizing the conflict. He is the great summarizer. Others see him as a compromiser.

• If you demand obedience to "your way," the **Conciliator** either will appear to acquiesce and then do what he wanted to do in the first place, get very resistant, or, worse, he will "fail" at the task you have ordered him to do. The empathy for your problems is gone when the focus is on his own activities. Unless you clearly spell out the roles you'll each have on the team, or the purpose of the project, and why the **Conciliator's** commitment is needed, personal feelings can and often do get in the way. Remember, this brainstyle hates being told what to do (it interferes with his internal controls of his own timing and feelings. It is then *personal.*) **Conciliators** like "direction," "clarity" and "support." You get the picture: let them figure out *how.*

• When the **Conciliator** forms an image of an outcome, a lot of left-brain dedication gets attached. This is the brainstyle reason why **Conciliators** *don't like to change* once they get committed to a direction.

Case in point: Don and Mary were entered in a golf tournament as a couple. Don, a **Conceptor,** had played in many tournaments over many years, and had a clear strategy for play. As they set out on the first hole he began telling Mary, a **Conciliator,** what to do. She balked. She slowed down. Don's face went red with the frustration of his game plan. He could <u>see</u> what to do. All Mary could "see" were his orders (the *relationship, right now*), and his red face, and she got madder and madder at being told what to do.

What saved the marriage was the "time out" Mary took, away from Don, as she walked to the first green. She realized she was mad and that it wasn't going to help her golf game (a focus on the goal). She then thought about Don's experience and his ability to strategize at golf better than she could. Settling down, she thought, "I *hate* the way he's talking to me (a focus on the interactions, her strength) but if I go along now, maybe I'll learn some things. I've *got* to change my focus. And I'll give him a piece of my mind *later.*" Her change in response to Don's next few instructions was faster. Don relaxed. Later they agreed that he had been impatient and spoken too harshly. ("My mind was totally on the goal, not your feelings.")

Mary said that she hadn't been given an overview of the gameplan — (made a part of the team) — so all of his directions were just his "bossiness." She resented this. He "seemed to be telling her she was stupid and couldn't figure things out for herself" (personalizing the information.)

They agreed to have a brief overview on how they would proceed the next time so Mary could have a clear role (be in control of how and what she did) on their team. *Neither expected the other to change.* They negotiated a context (being a "team") that could allow both to participate from their strengths.

Managing the Conciliator
• You must be aware that everything you say will first be "heard" by the right brain of the **Conciliator**. The enthusiasm and spontaneity that prompt the impromptu will automatically depend on an early positive reaction and be crushed by a negative one. Feedback will register personally. Establish a bigger context when presenting negative information; put what you're saying in perspective. <u>Slow down</u> with initial reactions or new information to give time for the **Conciliator's** left brain to catch up and be more objective. Ask — insist — that the **Conciliator** take time before responding.

Case in point: A new employee was nearly finished with a big project. She was so excited about her findings that on a chance meeting with her V.P. she decided to abandon protocol and give him a spontaneous preview of her conclusions.

"Do you have a minute?" she inquired. "I'd love to get your thoughts about the report before I cross all the 't's' and dot all the 'i's'."

Launching into a review of her main conclusions, she watched the V.P. get red in the face. Finally, she spluttered to a halt. "What's the matter?" she asked.

It seemed that her conclusions were **Time Zero** information for this V.P. Too late she realized that he also was a **Conciliator** brainstyle. He needed time to respond to new ideas which he instantly judged as "politically explosive," that would "put his budget in jeopardy." His reaction was not kind. To her, it was devastating. She was terribly embarrassed, and anxious about the VP's evaluation of her competence.

Afterward she realized that presenting touchy conclusions would have been much better *in a planned, structured setting* for both of them. She would have had time to anticipate his reactions instead of plunging in, expecting him to share her enthusiasm. *Timing* of her right-brain spontaneity would have done a lot to protect her feelings attached to the facts and prepare him as well. For their next meeting, she prepared a careful agenda, submitted a summary beforehand, and when the negative reactions appeared, she was prepared with alternatives. This put her in charge of facts and kept things from getting so personal.

• Rehearsal can be critical for **Conciliators**. No brainstyle can have higher aspirations or be more self-critical than the **Conciliator.** If the **Deliberator** wants to <u>be</u> it all, the **Conciliator** wants to *be and do* it all. This drive for perfection often translates into career ambition. Modify the **Conciliator's** drive by providing neutral facts *often* about performance to prevent a right-brain defined, *(rosy)* internal picture that doesn't include left-brain assessments (fact-based). This will take timing (two or three meetings, possibly) to allow for the **Conciliator's** right-brain, personal reactions.

• **Conciliators** want to get credit for their good work — without having to spell it out for all their unintuitive **Deliberator** or **Knower** superiors — that credit is definitely due. The **Conciliator** is ready to undertake great tasks for the greater good. What he is not prepared to do is to be denied recognition for it.

BrainStyle Clue:

*Beware: The **Conciliator** can be a dedicated workaholic who will do far more than he has been asked to do. Pay attention to what he is doing, because this extra work does not come for free. A **Conciliator** can become downright surly if he thinks he is not being appreciated in the way he would appreciate others. This surliness often gets expressed as demands for promotion or pay increases. **Conciliators** can quit on the spot or hold grudges.*

Here are some keys to the **Conciliator** that can be useful in helping those in that brainstyle find the right fit.

• Play to the strengths of **Conciliators** by putting them where they can deal with people.

• The **Conciliator** is the great enroller who can build the coalitions necessary to fulfilling a company's vision. The Conciliator activates a vision; he does not create one.

• Information is always personalized at **<u>Time Zero</u>** for **Conciliators**. Prepare them ahead for feedback, including performance appraisals, meetings, and large issues. Even after considering the information, many times they will still have more of a right-brain spin than other brainstyles.

• **Conciliators** make hasty decisions based purely on right-brain feelings. Instruct them to "think on it" before they give you their conclusions.

• The **Conciliator** most often will tell you what he thinks you want to hear — or stress the positives about a project — in an effort to make the day a little smoother. Don't ask the **Conciliator** to tell you the long-term downside — go to the **Deliberator** or the **Knower** for that.

• **Conciliators** have no immediate access to left-brain logic. Don't press for answers on new subjects that require it. Use them for imaginative assignments that require influencing, coordinating, training, selling — things that need bringing to life. For instance, *service* is a natural field for this brainstyle. When analysis and precision are required, it is best to allow time for preparation. If there is access to a **Deliberator** for proofreading or auditing all the better. This does not mean that **Conciliators** don't choose careers requiring skill in left-brained tasks — CPA's, professors, and technical **Conciliators** are numerous. Watch how they bring in others when getting the job done, however. Or how the task is personalized to include more meaning for others.

• **Conciliators** are the best of partners. If you want someone at your right hand who will promote your vision and work to make it happen, no other brainstyle is a more enthusiastic supporter.

• **Conciliators** take risks early. This is because they haven't considered the alternatives or the potential downsides (the "bad news"). They are best at figuring out how to "make it happen."

• No one is better at knowing on a feeling level what is happening *right now*. The **Conciliator** can do better at *meeting dynamics* than (new) meeting subjects.

• It might be helpful if every **Conciliator** wore a warning sign: "Caution! Please do not confuse imagination, visualizing abilities, and irrepressible enthusiasm with creating new directions, plans, or whole visions for the future." The **Conciliator's** gift for visualizing endless possibilities and alternatives for action is what suits this brainstyle. The **Conciliator** is best as a *doer*, a goal-setter and can be a real results-getter and can certainly image future plans in familiar areas of expertise. However, **Conciliators** are not *seers* (who can look ahead and see whole strategies or directions) in new areas. They sense their way along their own career paths. "I was just lucky," "I was in the right place at the right time," are typical answers to the question "How did you choose this career?"

• Finally, do not allow the feelings of this brainstyle to run the project or manipulate you or others into doing things you wouldn't ordinarily do. Feelings pass. They are rain clouds or sunshine, but they are not the reason for passing or taking on a project. If you are afraid of dealing with a **Conciliator** because of his or her **Time Zero** reaction, realize that if you don't make it so important, they will be through it and on to the real issue soon enough. Time is the problem. Time is the solution.

> *BrainStyle Clue:*
>
> *Although* **Conciliators** *may accept being told what to do, they are less willing to be told <u>how</u> to do it. Remember, figuring out <u>how</u> to get something done and getting others involved in it are the strengths of the* **Conciliator**. *Agree ahead of time on goals and roles to enroll the support of the* **Conciliator** *and then let him loose with some clear measures and reporting dates.*

For the two brainstyles influenced by the right brain, growing up means learning how to speak appropriately for the right brain, which has all those disconnected, off-the-wall emotional reactions.

When the **Conciliator** starts out, there are a great many personal, emotion-based needs which constantly influence decisions. Self-worth decisions are easily based on reactions from others — others give words to ambiguous right-brain messages. The gift for making relationships can easily become a judgment: When relationships don't work, the **Conciliator** decides he is not valuable. Yet positive self-esteem is developed from valuing one's gifts and knowing how they work regardless of the feedback. The **Conciliator** has to learn, as must each brainstyle, to be his or her own best fan from a very young age.

There is always a need for vision: the right brain *knows* — but the left brain figures out how to get there, building on logical past experience to create a real vision of the future. The **Conciliator,** using primarily right-brain input, basically feels and imagines his way along — sensing by what seems *right* (most often, *comfortable*) and how it might look to be there — in order to take the next job, or decide whom to work with. These people are excellent at turning ideas into goals (actions and defined results with time horizons), and figuring out alternatives and imaginative ways to get to the longer term where they will make people, imagination and feelings count.

• The **Conciliator** is a partner for success. The **Conciliator** works best when working in a partnership with one or more other people. Partners give the **Conciliator** a variety of (left-brain) opinions to work with and sort out. Partners provide support (right-brain). This ability to work within partnerships makes the **Conciliator** an ideal project manager. A well-defined project gives the **Conciliator** an arena, a stated goal, and a group of people to influence. What could be better? Such a set-up lets **Conciliators** get the attention they like. They can move the project. And *that* can be very good for business.

• When two **Conciliators** work together, however, the collaboration can be difficult because of their strengths: too much understanding, too much positive feedback, too much of the relationship and not enough confrontation and clarity. Everything is personal. Either plan for regular task reviews or, better yet, have access to another brainstyle to bring in a left-brain perspective.

• If you are working for a **Conciliator,** negotiate some ways you can contribute to your boss's personal sense of just how good this business can be, including adding the downside to get the whole picture.

• The **Conciliator** cares how you feel about your work and your life — and expects you to return the interest. Explain how *you* show that you appreciate her efforts so you can reach an understanding that isn't personal.

• Unless an important question requires an immediate answer, ask your **Conciliator** manager to take time to think it over. Give time for the left-brain review. The second-best strategy is to wait a little while and then confirm the response.

• When the **Conciliator** makes a request of you (or asks a favor), treat it carefully. Ask a lot of questions about real expectations. Try to pin down the specifics in a way that helps her get clear on what she wants. Behind the casual request often lies the friendly command.

• The **Conciliator** is the one who can <u>do</u> what needs to be done — and is likely to expect (assume) you will pitch in and do the same. The friendliness can rapidly turn icy if you do not fulfill the unvoiced expectations. The danger here is that when the resentment is unexpressed, it feeds on itself and grows. **Conciliators** can shut down and then get even. You need to ask what their expectations are.

• Do not misread **Conciliators** as "softies." Because they are in touch with the right brain does not mean they are warm fuzzies all the time. The over-achieving **Conciliator** can be an impatient, critical, hard-working perfectionist. When a **Conciliator** is in motion, realize that you are seeing commitment to an ideal in action. The **Conciliator** can come across as uncaring and pushy.

• The **Conciliator** has trouble giving direct, negative feedback no matter how she may brag beforehand that she can handle it. The truth is that confronting someone is personally uncomfortable and the **Conciliator** brings too many feelings to the situation.

• Prepare the **Conciliator** for change *beforehand.* These people get attached to their image of the future and hate to let it go. It will take several conversations to replace the old image with a new one. **Conciliators** want to know the benefits for <u>them</u>.

The Deliberator at Work

The special gift of the **Deliberator** is assessing — against personally developed standards (what is "right"). Drawing on learning and experience, the **Deliberator** creates "models" (descriptions of what has already gone before, assessed as "right"). These models can be useful for describing or explaining (making sense of) complex businesses. And professors do just this. A clear list of standards can also be mistaken for the company's *vision* of the future. In other words, **Deliberator** models are useful for naming criteria for future decisions *based on past experience.* They provide continuity. They provide a new look at existing ideas. They do not make <u>new</u> decisions about the unknown, new situations in the future. Economists, often bright **Deliberators,** tell us the future with a ruler: extend the line ahead based on what has gone before.

• The **Deliberator** creates systems and executes plans. He does not see over the horizon or make up the totally new the way the **Conceptor** does or attack the new project with the rapidity and decisiveness of the **Knower.**

• The **Deliberator,** a natural information processor, can *assess a situation rapidly* to determine whether it is on track, missing something, or needs attention. This can create a solid direction in which to proceed. It is not the same as the future view of the **Conceptor,** which can define *possibilities,* which often are illogical and risky. The pictures these two brainstyles define are quite distinct. One is logical and a synergy of information. One is illogical and speculative. The **Deliberator** is at his best when applying his abilities to refine, describe, and work out the details of putting a *vision* into operation.

Case in point: Frank is a financial consultant who worked nine years for Arthur Andersen. He built his reputation on his ability to go into a company — even one with unfamiliar technology — and figure out how to make it more profitable. Frank has been extremely successful by using his **Deliberator** strengths to their fullest. As an experienced auditor and business assessor, Frank has "memory banks" that are loaded with the essential criteria for financial success. His data base is broad and applicable to a variety of businesses.

Frank's keen and constant assessments come from his ability to collect, sort and remember details in an organized way, details that become criteria for successful businesses. *It is critical that the* **Deliberator** *have good data to assess and file away because he works with what already exists.* He compares the actual situation (reflected in the company's books and employee interviews) with his previously determined and tested standards for success. Thus he applies a "model" or formula: compare the standard (what it should be) *vs.* the actual (what it is today), name the gaps, and make recommendations for revisions. The business gets corrected, stabilized.

The future will look like the past (other stable companies) refracted through the present. **Deliberators** will bring stability and measured improvements to a system when they apply their abilities of collecting and assessing. *Experience* (more chances to use their brainstyle) is *essential* for effectiveness.

Frank's aim is *not* to create a new direction for the company he is reviewing [as the **Conceptor** would do]. He <u>may</u> prescribe more efficient ways to shape things up [as the **Knower** would], however. Frank's most natural approach is to question and offer counsel on how the existing system might be improved or made more efficient *within the boundaries* of the company's vision for itself.

> *BrainStyle Clue:*
> *Once the vision exists, the* **Deliberator** *can plan how to get there. The gift of the* **Deliberator** *shows up best in assessing, reorganizing and improving.*

• The major management *non-strength* of the **Deliberator** is delegation. In fact, the **Deliberator's** great ability to collect data, nail down standards for success, and then project those standards into the future makes it very difficult for this brainstyle to truly delegate. Making an accurate projection depends on having all of the information lined up like a row of beans. But if some of that information has been delegated away for others to work on, then there will be gaps in that great highway into the future. Simply put, a **Deliberator** cannot look at and assess all the pieces if all the pieces are not there.

When faced with the task of delegation, the **Deliberator** has three options: delegate none of it, delegate all of it, or make piece work of it all.

Typically, the **Deliberator** takes the first path. When in charge, this brainstyle is constantly referred to as "very controlling" by subordinates. Often in the early stages of planning, he may assign fact-finding tasks to others — but only as a means of assembling data. These assignments don't amount to delegation because they do not carry with them any bottom-line responsibility. The assignments can have a lot of people busy who do not have the whole picture of what everyone else is doing. Hence, duplication. Inefficiency. Cost overruns.

The less typical way for the **Deliberator** to stay close to all of the data is (1) to set up a management system that farms out *everything* to a large staff or (2) to meet with that staff often and long so everyone is "reading from the same page."

Cases in point:

Case I: Robert Crandall of American Airlines

Mr. Crandall, dubbed "detail monger" by *Fortune* magazine, has exploited his **Deliberator** strengths of amassing "the tiniest details," assessing, refining, and probing into a precise execution to ensure that American Airlines' systems are the best — and in fact have been the basis for a large part of American's success.[5] His planning meetings have become legend in the industry. He has a large staff and portions out to them all the pieces for devising a planning strategy. He uses frequent meetings to interrogate his fact finders, relentlessly probing them for every last detail of their research. Creativity is out of the question, say subordinates. The systems are then aligned and those in charge of each one can execute their plan — after a line-by-line scrutiny.

The innovation and steady progress of American Airlines was the big success story of the '80s. How? *Get it, assess it, challenge it, sort it, mark it, divide it, plan it. Step by step. Cover all the bases. One step at a time...with continual connection to the customer to ensure the best data to feed into the loop.* And Crandall leads the way with his endless energy and attention to detail.

Tough? The good news and the bad news are Crandall's relentless pursuit of information, his domination of his endless meetings, his constant assessment of any idea until it is broken into its tiniest parts and he seems to be the only one who can put the pieces together. What is the secret to his success? The relentless process focuses on a very competitive goal, and there is enough input to move it forward with commitment from the many, not just the few. His boundless energy allows for an enormous amount of small decisions to be made at the most senior levels. No, he doesn't delegate; he challenges, leaves you to it, and then challenges some more, say American employees. And, they say, "Yes, he is a very talented businessman, but then *he isn't very good with people."*

Does the brainstyle of the critics really allow them to see the truth about Crandall? This is an example of gossip clearly based on brainstyle. There will not really be an appreciation of any leader, no matter how talented or how well the company does, when people criticize performance based on their own strengths. There is no way to really win by focusing on Crandall's non-strength.

American Airlines with Crandall at the helm, like the Japanese or Steve Bostic (described in Chapter Six), has advanced steadily and relentlessly into the marketplace, driven by his **Deliberator** planning process, positively glacial in its progress, its thoroughness, and its apparent inevitability. This does not mean that it is slow to take place. Many can be engaged in frenzied activity over long periods. What it can produce are the SABRE Reservation System and the leading Frequent Flyer program — the results of endless meetings chaired by Crandall at which ideas and data eventually become new products. In both cases AMR ended up setting the standard, making the rules. Bob Crandall didn't invent either one of them. But he certainly is in charge of a system that did.

It is interesting to note the critique of Bob Crandall's lack of "people skills" for an even broader reason. As the **Deliberator** brainstyle does not naturally address people issues first or best, nor does any brainstyle address *their non-strengths.* The real problem is the expectation some American Airlines employees as well as most of the American public have of leaders: To be gifted in *all four strengths.* This is perfection. Leaders are human. Limitless thinking is being applied in the wrong area.

• **Deliberator** cultures thrive on analysis before action — the strength of the brainstyle — and last the longest when they do it well. Steady as she goes. There are many systems, rules and procedures to keep the even keel. The point is, when the top leadership runs the company in a way that is *comfortable,* and *controlled,* the horizons shrink and synergy gets lost. The CEO **Deliberator** Roger Smith proposes rational, technological solutions to the decline of General Motors. He speaks of his middle management as "obstacles" to progress. The maverick entrepreneur, H. Ross Perot confronts Smith with a need to manage people differently to get the most out of them. How can a very rational, large company with **Deliberator** leadership renew itself? This is the question for many leaders of both large firms and small departments. It cannot be answered by a single brainstyle.

One thing we need to focus on presently, however, is that the brainstyle (micro) of the leader will predict the culture (macro) of the business.

Case II: The Inexperienced Deliberator

Ron, a new production manager, is a **Deliberator** not yet clear on how to apply his strengths and, therefore, unable to focus or deliver on what he promises. He spends time collecting information about the problems of his plant, which is indeed in bad shape. (Assessing gaps.) He talks a great deal about his big plans for the future. (Creating models based on past experience.) Approaching problems with a focus on the detail means that all problems have nearly equal importance. He sets goals in accordance with his desire to fix everything he has assessed. There are no real priorities. There are no decisions, because there is no overall clarity, and therefore there is very little focused action. There *is* a lot of activity. There *is* a demand for more information in order to keep control in the hands of the guy at the top. Getting approvals replaces making decisions. There is a line outside Ron's office waiting to discuss and get the go-ahead on a basketful of problems, one at a time. The differences between Crandall and Ron are interesting: Ron's boss would say the difference is one of self-confidence. Ron is unsure of himself (a right-brain problem) and can't decide to move forward. Another assessment is that his experience and background (stored memory) does not match the current assignment, so that he can not apply what he knows — perhaps the crucial factor for this brainstyle.

Ron was finally transferred to a technical function (a job he had held before), with fewer direct reports, where he could provide planning support — a job that used the same strengths and more closely matched his experience. In getting the product scheduled, formulated, and in line with customer specifications, he was successful. The tasks were fewer and more complex; his strengths at assessing and planning could be applied incisively to specific projects. He was no longer managing untrained people, or a system with huge numbers of **Time Zero** events demanding decisions in new areas. Everyone was happier. And more productive. Ron stayed with the company as a real contributor for many years. Without the change, he surely would have been fired, losing both self-esteem and clarity about what his real contribution to a company needed to be.

> *BrainStyle Clue:*
> *Experience is everything for a* **Deliberator***. Action is based on what is already stored in memory. A steady progression of jobs is vital for incremental improvements — in abilities, and in results. Don't expect a* **Deliberator** *to handle a job with too many* **Time Zero** *events within deadlines.*

One way to compare Mr. Crandall and Ron is to compare their abilities to handle quantities of data (stored experience), their energy level, and consequently, their results. The scope of their endeavors is quite different. The brainstyles of both men are the same.

Research suggests that the speed of processing information predicts "intelligence."[6] What it means for the individual is that the faster the processing, the more bits of information that get stored. Crandall may indeed process information faster. That's the hardware. The decision that Ron may have made about his own abilities (the lack of self-confidence that his boss suspected) which can shut down an ability to learn and take chances can certainly be changed. And, we suspect, it is this kind of a decision that may just allow the opening up of new "storage space" in the brain. When a person feels "confident" it is likely that there have been decisions made that allow the brain to do its job easier and faster.

What is important for the organization is understanding the basic strengths of the individual to create the right "job fit." This will do the most toward building confidence — in the case of **Deliberators,** so they are free to apply their stored data and experience — and enable them to expand their abilities on their own.

BrainStyle Clue:
Deliberators *are often the "naysayers" in the group. They* <u>*assess first.*</u> *They sound negative. The brainstyle looks for "gaps" (problems in the system) — and needs time to repair them. This can delay the action. Seek them out to tell you what is or might go wrong in your plan.*

• In general, then, the **Deliberator** is happiest *perfecting* — the system, the company or himself. He does not like dealing with the conceptual or the irrational — especially if it isn't (or can't be) tied down to reality in writing. Thus the IBM personal computer had to be developed by a maverick group immune to the IBM corporate culture and its **Deliberator** motto: THINK. To the **Deliberator**, being able to articulate an idea clearly in writing is a sure sign of having a good idea. Yet for all his clarity of articulation, the **Deliberator's** strength is not in making breakthroughs. The **Deliberator's** strengths kick in *after* the criteria of the breakthrough have been articulated.

Case in point: Gerry, a **Deliberator**, is a distribution manager for a consumer products firm. When management announced that reducing costs was the #1 priority, Gerry set about responding to the challenge (executing a plan once the vision is established). He assessed that the first "gap" was in controlling warehousing expenses. The sales function had always managed warehousing. Their mandate was and is to satisfy customer needs. Costs came second in most decisions.

In presenting his case to his new **Conceptor** boss, Gerry demonstrated with facts and figures, as well as a field trip, how much cheaper it would be to bring warehousing under his control. He pointed out how sales overspent. As he lobbied with his boss and other peers, Gerry was told he "came across negatively." His appeal to reason only sounded self-serving (do this because it's cheaper, and I can handle it better). He followed the Deliberator's process: here's the standard (lower costs); here's where you're losing money (the gap), and here's the recommendation: put distribution in charge — a very logical process, but not carried out in a very *political, i.e., making everyone a winner,* interpersonal strategy.

The discussion between Gerry and his **Conceptor** boss quickly identified a strategy to use in presenting the excellent data, which could persuade with reason and also address the bigger picture: the several functions that would be affected — especially sales. The difference? Right-brain input that addressed the feelings of the teed-off sales group which saw someone after its turf.

Once the rational and emotional reasons had been named and addressed, a strategy was developed to get support for the change, a strategy that included more people in the solution. What is important to notice here is that *Gerry didn't even see the problems generated by his strategy at first.* This is because of brainstyle, not because of *intelligence.*

Gerry learned a great deal about "politics" (a non-strength) and "networking" as a part of the task to be done, which is how a **Deliberator** can easily approach the people issues in a complex project. These "right-brain" items need to get on the list. They won't get there as a rule, unless the **Deliberator** gets other's input or has put other groups in his plan from the start.

Gerry has established a new agenda to address organizational problems — based on discussions with his **Conceptor** boss. After learning about Gerry's brainstyle, the boss asked Gerry to address the concept of "service." Gerry defined "service" as a step-by-step program to be implemented *with* sales. The strengths of each brainstyle were maximized: the **Conceptor's** ability to define a problem globally, and the **Deliberator's** ability to define and execute an incremental, measurable plan.

Finding the Fit

As the brainstyle with the natural gift for learning, the **Deliberator** looks "mature" early. He is more controlled, more rational, and less reactive than are other brainstyles. He most often excels in school and has the best grades, then the best resumes. This is both the good news and the bad news. He is expected to achieve a lot. And he often does. However, he does not <u>excel</u> in the areas of other brainstyles — and this is what we often expect of him: to be all things to all people.

Keep in mind the **Deliberator's <u>non</u>-strengths** — managing with:
• **Time Zero** decisions;
• Creativity;
• Spontaneity, reacting quickly with empathy;
• Flexibility to change the plan in mid-course (which is very **different than adding new information,** revising the decision, or keeping open to additional information — this non-strength of the **Deliberator** is the strength of the **Conceptor**, literally starting over and *trying out a whole new plan*);
• Risk taking;
• Establishing clear priorities in a **new area**, defining the Big Picture or direction to follow in the future (as distinct from synthesizing facts or previous information into a clear focus or model of how it can be based on what exists *now* — a **Deliberator** strength);
• Confrontation, especially direct, face-to-face or regarding the larger business issues.

Deliberators will not be as gifted in these areas as other brainstyles. Don't expect them to be.

The Creative Mix

As we've seen, each of the four brainstyles possesses unique strengths and non-strengths. It follows, then, that all four will be required in the highest-performing companies.

> [The] United States has an industrial infrastructure that should be unbeatable. America has fifteen million companies (no other nation comes close) and 5.5 million scientists and engineers (two times the number in Japan), and we have won more Nobel prizes than the rest of the world together. We spend twice as much on R&D as Germany and Japan combined.[7]

There is only one problem with the above statement: infrastructures don't make breakthroughs; people do. *We must energize the infrastructure — the vast wealth of businesses and their assets — with the right people working together and doing the right jobs.*

BrainStyle Application Section

BrainStyle Application #2

In the preceding chapter you read how different brainstyles interact. In order to work with others based on openly stated strengths, the following exercise may be helpful. It has been used as a discussion outline for people who need to work together and learn a new way of discussing expectations with one another.

A *Strength Contract* is an outline for you to present and receive information about what you do naturally and best in the context of your work.

If the other person is not familiar with *brainstyles,* help them identify strengths in their own words, using brainstyle definitions to give focus. The format is open-ended enough that you might use it in your own words, of course, as a way to negotiate with others on an ongoing basis.

A BrainStyle Exercise

A Strengths Contract

ME

My brainstyle strengths are _____

_____

My values and standards for performance are _____

_____

YOU

Your brainstyle strengths are _____

_____

Your values and standards for performance are _____

_____

WORK

Where we are interdependent in our work is _____

_____

PLAN

I will time my requests of you so that _____

_____

You will time your requests of me so that _____

_____

We can include strengths other than our own by _____

_____

Chapter Eight

Where You Can Take Your BrainStyle

CHAPTER EIGHT

WHERE YOU CAN TAKE YOUR BRAINSTYLE

Confronting Your Limits

The biggest waste of our time and energy comes from a double error. *Error #1: We do not identify and develop our natural strengths.* In trying to grow or learn, we have misused our strengths to adapt, to "flex," to go along to get ahead. We lose our maximum impact. *Error #2: We focus on improving our non-strengths.* We compete with others by trying to do what *they* can do well and we cannot. We correct ourselves, trying hard to shore up our "weaknesses," and end up putting tremendous effort learning things we can only marginally improve. The double loss produces mediocre results in both areas. We get ourselves coming and going.

We have confused ourselves on the most fundamental of levels. Our spirit — our capacity to give, to love, to commit to others — is *unlimited*. Our mental hardware — the way we process information to decide, learn, express — is *limited*. We set ourselves up with role models and criteria which define "success." We cannot help but feel inadequate and judge ourselves against these measures as *not good enough.*

Do you want to continue doing things the same way you've always done them?

The first step is the hardest: <u>you</u> start by coming to terms with your strengths and non-strengths. This is simple, but not easy. For some of us, to accept limits of any kind is a blow to our most precious investment: Who We Want to Become. To accept that you are *already there* — <u>right where you are</u> — is to give up an enormous effort of striving and trying in fruitless areas. The truth of our lives is that we are limited in *how* we learn, but unlimited in *what* we can learn. We get the two confused.

The conversation about strengths and non-strengths must be a very caring one. It starts with what you say to yourself. It continues in what you say to others. Defensiveness falls away when you already know what others are going to say about your "good" and "bad" sides. You can tell *them*. The ace up your sleeve is owning your strengths and non-strengths.

You know people like this: they're content with themselves, (not the situation), they're powerful, they enter any situation from a baseline of self confidence.

A BrainStyle Review

You are limited. You have a basic set of strengths based on your brainstyle. You cannot change the way you process information.

You are unlimited. You have an unlimited capacity to master your strengths. You have a near limitless capacity in what you can learn and recall when you work from strength. You have an unlimited ability to love, to care, to give to others, to realize success.

You take your strengths for granted, and tend to focus on non-strengths or times when you use effort. Your brainspeed is at maximum, yet you are the *least aware* of it, when you are using your **natural strengths**. Recently, brain imaging researchers at UCLA reported results from measuring the energy expended by the brain when two groups of people took an IQ test. The higher scorers were predicted to use more energy and more of their brain (based undoubtedly on the old maxim that "we're only using some 10% of our brain") as they took the test. In fact, *just the opposite* occurred:

> Those who performed best on the IQ test tended, on average, to produce 'cooler,' more subdued [brain] scan patterns...while their less intellectually gifted counterparts lit up like miniature Christmas trees....The brain of the less intelligent person seemed to have to work harder to achieve less.[1]

This research substantiates why natural strengths are effortless — and we strain to do what is <u>not</u> comfortable or natural.

As we have asserted, and science is just now establishing, your natural gifts are the fastest and easiest use of your mental hardware. Those "less intellectually gifted" who were being measured in the UCLA study were, we must assume, *gifted in some other way* — and so when using a non-strength showed strain, expending a great deal of energy.

You are not a combination of brainstyles. You have a multitude of <u>behaviors</u> that can look like what someone in another brainstyle looks like when they are using their strengths. The difference is, when it is a non-strength of yours, you cannot sustain the ability nor do you ever reach mastery with that behavior. Comparing yourself to yourself, you may observe creativity, quick, logical decisions, and analytical skills. But when you work with someone else who is gifted in one of the other strength areas, you quickly realize that you do not have the ease or gifts that they have in that brainstyle area.

Others will not really appreciate or understand what your real strengths are. Stop waiting for them to do so. You are <u>least understood</u> when you are <u>at your best</u>, most excited, most creative, most practical — most *yourself.* As your brain functions fast and effortlessly, only someone who has the same brainstyle, or someone who has made it his or her business to gain from what you have to offer will "track" how you are thinking — if they are interested.

You <u>can</u> change your attitudes, values, opinions. You cannot change your brainstyle, but you can change what you have stored in your memory. Previous decisions which influence your beliefs about the way you view the world can, with <u>work</u> (counseling, psychotherapy or personal insight) change. That is, you can revisit old decisions and revise your attitude about what you have stored, or even the content. Many of us, in remembering an incident from childhood that at the time seemed traumatic, have been able to look at the incident from an adult perspective and literally see the incident with a new meaning. The problem is getting access to these memories. *You have filed memories as you processed them.* This means that if you take in experiences in detail, you will recall them with detail. And unearthing what you have long filed, used, and now access through well-used neural pathways is quite a process. And people of other brainstyles, who process information differently than you do, cannot access your "files" easily, if at all. That is why therapies work voluntarily. The person perceives it is much more painful to act from what is stored in memory than to make a new decision in order to believe and act in a new way.

Instead of demanding someone else change, use brainstyle <u>timing</u> to enhance communications. In studying relationships between different brainstyles, the most important factor in creating rapport seems to be *brainspeed.* People who have a similar energy level or pace of processing information seem to be able to communicate more easily than where one is faster than the other. This implies that *understanding* can be greatly improved if we *time interactions* instead of beating each other up with demands for changes in the way we communicate. Besides, waiting for another to see things as you do is to give your power to them. Put that power into expressing your strengths more effectively.

No brainstyle is better than any other. Each brainstyle has its good news and bad news. How could any one brainstyle be best? The best brainstyle is the one that fits the particular need, or job. Stop competing by comparing yourself to others. You are best at being you. Let others be themselves.

How Effective Do You Want To Be?

Many people resist new ideas by first trying to prove that they were right in the way they have always done things. You may be most comfortable with a behavioral approach, so you will use the four categories of brainstyles to find where you fit, classify your friends, and quit before anything serious happens. If by now you haven't gotten clear that *The BrainStyles System*™ is one you must apply differently to yourself and to others before you receive the real benefits, we hope to make it clear now.

Three Places To Test Your BrainStyle

If you are willing to give up the search for perfection, e.g., mastering the strengths of all four brainstyles, and focus on your own set of gifts, there are three areas that may test your self-acceptance against your ambition. **Creativity. Entrepreneurship. Leadership.** There is a multi-million dollar industry telling us that we can learn how to succeed in all of these areas if we study, practice and try their seminars. If *you* have a focus, you will know where you can grow and what to do if you <u>cannot learn</u> what they are trying to teach. Knowing and applying your gifts takes honest self appraisal and partnerships that are based on the same.

1. *Stop trying to learn to be creative* — if this is not your strength.

There are two broad categories of <u>results</u> in the area of bringing forth new ideas:

> *Creativity* is the process that creates *something out of <u>nothing</u>*. The result is a breakthrough. This happens infrequently and unpredictably.

> *Innovation* is the process that makes *something out of <u>something.</u>* The result is an *incremental improvement*. This happens in a much more predictable sequence, although solutions can appear as spontaneous and intuitive. They are really the result of research and informed procedures.

It's important to know the difference in the results you or someone else can produce when making a career choice, hiring someone, or structuring a research department. It is not important if you are looking for education on the subject or a seminar to improve attitudes about new ideas.

Take the logic of any technology already available — from micro chips to music to marine paint — and make it better. Maybe you can make it better by 5 to 15 percent. Improving something 5 to 15 percent — especially if you can do it on a consistent basis, is awesome — world class. Just *don't call the improvement a "creation."* It is incremental improvement, and the basis for most technological advances.

Creativity, however, leads to *breakthroughs* — leaps in technology or thinking — where there is no proof, rationale, or precedent, to create something that was not there before.

Wilbur and Orville Wright made a breakthrough. The Stealth bomber is an incremental improvement. The Leitz camera was a breakthrough. The Minolta SX 7000 is an incremental improvement. You get the picture.

You need *both*.

We do not know how to nurture either of these processes to excellence because we are all trying to learn how to do them both. This just doesn't work.

Observe the differences when contrasting the processes and their results in the following chart:

BREAKTHROUGH CREATIVITY	**INCREMENTAL IMPROVEMENT**
• Creates **something of value** (not just ideas) from *nothing*	• Makes something **better** from something that exists
• Makes a leap	• Takes a step
• An illogical process, with lots of right-brain input that has no data or proof behind it	• A logical process with much left-brain research to substantiate decisions
• Can produce up to 100% change, right now. Occurs at irregular, spontaneous intervals	• Can produce a 5-15% improvement at once, show measurable progress, and over time, can result in a 100% or more improvement

BrainStyle Fact #1: *Breakthrough creativity cannot be taught and cannot be learned.* Brain*speed* and brain*processing* cannot be changed, only enhanced. Creating breakthroughs depends on how the brain works, and as you now appreciate, brains work according to brainstyles.

Those brainstyles capable of breakthrough creativity must have

access to the right brain inputs of irrational, illogical ideas —
beyond the sensing and testing of the immediate environment. Both
Conceptors and **Conciliators** have this access. **Conciliators'** gifts
do not include the same balance of left-brain input however.
Conciliators sense, feel, imagine, intuit as they *draw from previous
experience*. **Conceptors** envision, strategize and test and have the
capacity to leave previous experience behind.

The **Deliberators** and **Knowers** are best at coming up with new
ways to apply existing ideas in the future. They make sense — and
they get to vital new places in mainly practical or rational steps.

Myth #1: *Creativity Can Be Learned.* Work done in the area of
"whole brain research" says that with various exercises and classes
you can expand your capacity to use more of your abilities. (See
Appendix A) Seminars in creativity advertise that "anyone who
learns to unleash the potential of the right brain can learn to be
creative." *Hogwash.* You *can* learn techniques (like brainstorming or
making analogies) that improve how you come up with new ideas in
order to incrementally improve the idea or product. You *can
improve your attitude* and *make new decisions* about what you
consider as valid ideas by drawing upside down or writing with the
opposite hand. This may be the best way to bring the gifts of the
right-brained into the world of science — and may lead to more
breakthroughs. Many have discovered their own gifts this way, or
just had a great time. But do not confuse new *skills* with *brainstyle*.
You will use and apply skills according to what you do naturally.

"Creativity" as defined by Ned Herrmann, author of *The Creative
Brain,*[2] is very broad:

> Creativity is an ability to challenge assumptions,
> recognize patterns, see in new ways, and relate the
> previously unrelated.[3]

If you put things together in new ways, you can be creative.
According to this definition, all brainstyles can be creative. It is now
unacceptable to not be part of the group called "creative."

As part of the culture at large, where everyone is expected to be good at everything, everyone in business is expected to come up with "new ways to process information" or "relate the previously unrelated." *But brainstyles process information and make connections in markedly different ways with vastly different processes and even more divergent results.* We must stop expecting everyone to do the same things if only we can train them or fix them up with new technologies. Apply the technologies to strengths. You can be awesomely powerful if you can be awesomely clear on your strengths and non-strengths.

BrainStyles and Creativity in Business

Corporate America is largely run by **Deliberators** and **Knowers** and supported by **Deliberators** and **Conciliators**. Look around if you want proof. This is neither bad nor good — except when the top *unconsciously* duplicates itself, filling the management ranks with those who make them comfortable with a methodical, rational approach rather than those who can create tension, insights, and *breakthroughs*. This does not prevent individuals nor companies from continuing to demand breakthroughs from those who cannot deliver them. Or demanding a rational, quantifiable process from those who must stretch to do so. Notice that the two brainstyles most likely to be missing from the top are **Conceptors** and **Conciliators** — both of whom provide imaginative right-brain input at **Time Zero** without training.

Deliberators and **Knowers** do not process information in ways that lead to breakthroughs. They have other strengths which drive progress and serve industry enormously well. Neither one of them has immediate access to the imaginative right brain, and without imagination, *as a strength,* there is little possibility of creating something out of nothing.

How do you reach mastery in creativity? Or in finding new ways to do old things? Certainly you must assess, then develop those gifts you already have, naturally. You may have to start by letting go of past labels like *creative* or *rational.*

Here is one of many possible applications of brainstyles in business to foster creativity and focus more effectively on innovation.

1. Assess the brainstyles of your team, department, or company.

2. Structure meetings and teams differently for *incremental improvements* vs. *breakthroughs* on critical projects or issues. Draw on an experienced **Conceptor** and partner her or him with one or more **Conciliators** to work on the front-end of a task that needs to break new ground. Use training in *creativity* to focus the processes of the creative **Conceptors** and imaginative **Conciliators** so they can collaborate more effectively, and at the right time with the **Deliberators** and **Knowers**.

3. Create a supportive climate for two different groups: *Breakthroughs* and *Innovators* (incremental improvers). Right-brained folks often respond to wide-open spaces and empty white boards and unstructured times to work in. It will look "unprofessional" perhaps. But this is nothing new. The regular work spaces will make up for it, staying organized and structured for incremental updates and reports.

Whether you are the CEO, a supervisor, or individual contributor, you will expand your influence with the company or team as you look for ways to apply what you do naturally for those around you, and support others in doing the same.

Area #2 for testing your ambitions: *Entrepreneurship*.

Anyone can start a new business. There are tens of thousands started in the U.S. each year. Yet there is only the Inc. 100 — the fastest growing, most successful of the lot. And of that 100, only a handful are left at the end of a decade.

Why? Are people lazy? Stupid? Slow learners? Are we ignoring the vast sea of books and magazines on How To Succeed At Anything You Want To Do? Why haven't more of us learned how to be creative or start a winning venture?

Because creativity and entrepreneurship cannot be learned.

Because natural gifts can improve with study to become excellent and acquired skills can at best produce competence.

How can you assess whether you will make it as an entrepreneur? Most look to the experience (what the person can contribute out of stored memory) of the person proposing a start up. The resume is the sole reference point. But, as you now know, it is the **Time Zero** strengths that will make all the difference.

How honest can you be in assessing your own potential?

Jerry White and John Welsh, co-authors of *The Entrepreneur's Master Planning Guide,* have done extensive research to create a profile of successful entrepreneurs.[4] It closely resembles that of a high-energy, mature **Conceptor**. A **Knower** will also fit — provided the business is not a people-intensive one. Welsh and White notice that the *successful entrepreneurs do not do well in large corporations.* They observe, moreover, that *those who do well in large corporations do not do well as entrepreneurs* — e.g., H. Ross Perot, very successful as head of EDS, his own venture, and, after being bought out by General Motors, a poor fit for the Board of GM. Further, they note that *those who succeed in their own ventures and who do not have all the characteristics listed below usually have someone influencing their judgment who is strong in the characteristics in which they are weak.* So if you know your brainstyle, you may be able to start a business and pick the right partner because of their strengths rather than their resume.

The successful entrepreneur, according to White and Welsh, is characterized by:

1. Good health — the will to be well and stay on the job.
2. A basic need to control and direct — not to be confused with a need for power over people — a need for freedom to create and execute strategies they see as necessary.

3. Self-confidence — in her own abilities, when she is in control, and in the face of adversity. When she is not in control her involvement and constructive participation

diminishes.

4. Never-ending sense of urgency — to do something, to accomplish; impatient and tense with inactivity.

5. Comprehensive awareness — of how the specifics fit into her overall plans; how the single event fits the distant vision.

6. Realistic — neutral about facts and news, looks at information as it furthers the goal — wants to constantly measure and be measured; says what she means and keeps her word with people; in tune with the status of things.

7. Superior conceptual ability — entrepreneurs identify relationships among functions and things quickly in the midst of complex and confused situations; quick to identify the problem and begin working on the solution faster than other people around them. Their achievement orientation and their problem-solving ability overwhelm obstacles.

8. Low need for status personally rather than for her business; she can admit 'I don't know' and her ego doesn't get in the way of asking for others' data or guidance.

9. Objective approach to interpersonal relationships — a focus on the accomplishments rather than the feelings; a tendency to be more distant psychologically. To start up the enterprise, they are apparently insensitive to others. Those with better interpersonal skills last longer.

10. Sufficient emotional stability — even though she frequently has strong emotional feelings and reactions, she is able to be self-controlled, and is challenged by setbacks; tends to counsel others with action plans rather than focusing on

her own feelings.

11. Attraction to challenges, not risks — she assesses risks, then acts; she wishes to influence the outcome, not tackle the impossible.[5]

The size of the company each brainstyle CEO can competently bring to profitable success varies. **Conciliators** do well with smaller companies. **Deliberators** and **Knowers** can manage more complexity. The problems start when there is a need to add additional levels of management. Then the people issues kick in: delegation and dealing with conflict. These three brainstyles do not naturally handle **Time Zero** issues in these areas well. Both **Conciliators** and **Deliberators** must especially address #5 above: "the ability to balance the details with the vision — with the emphasis just beyond the horizon." All of these issues grow geometrically as the business expands.

As Professor White found with successful entrepreneurs, they supplement their non-strengths with someone else's strengths. This means that a key application of *The BrainStyles System*™ is setting up and growing entrepreneurial partnerships or teams. Jack Welch, when promoted as a young **Conceptor** to be head of General Electric, was made part of a trio by his wise predecessor, to balance his strengths.

Do <u>you</u> fit the profile of the successful entrepreneur? Many business people with good ideas start companies several times during their careers. Usually the reason for failure is blamed on externals: the product, pricing, the location, the economy, competition or funding. It is too difficult to really assess the leadership and what is missing from its ability to lead. **Deliberators** can be very strong building or redirecting *existing* businesses, **Conciliators** work best in smaller, people-intensive or imaginative fields. **Knowers** do well at start-ups or turn-arounds, but have a hard time after the initial phase, unless, like the **Knower** Perot, they have loyal lieutenants (**Deliberators**) running the company for the long haul (EDS, Perot's company built in Dallas and acquired by General Motors is an example). **Conceptors** have the closest potential fit with the entrepreneur's profile. Yet they take seasoning, working and learning the specifics — mastering the skills of a field — in order to mature.

Can you empower others to execute your ideas? There is a very short time in the early stages of a business when you must direct it yourself. Most entrepreneurs who get trapped by their need to control fail.

Do you know your strengths well enough to select the right partner? The best opportunity with the wrong person can be worse than a bad marriage. Knowing your strengths and non-strengths is critical in order to answer these questions.

> Myth #2: *Anyone Can Be an Entrepreneur if they have the right idea at the right time and can get the capital.*

> BrainStyle fact #2: *BrainStyle is a determining factor in the type and size of entrepreneurial venture you take on successfully.*

The third area to assess is *Leadership.*

In the opening chapter we quoted professor Bennis who has studied leaders in many walks of life to conclude "To be a leader, you must become yourself, the maker of your own life."

How will <u>you</u> go about doing this?

Myth #3: *You Can Learn to be a Leader.*

This mandate of business schools says that there really is a right way to lead and you must fit the model to succeed. They propose to teach you.

What if we agreed that there really is only one or two characteristics that are necessary for a *leader*, and then stopped making it better to be one?

There is a different function required of the top spot: to look out over the horizon, scan the field and figure out the direction. This cannot be taught.

The one in charge defines and greatly influences the culture of the team, and ultimately, the company. This influence does not mean the person necessarily has the vision of a *leader*. Yet the responsibility and impact is profound when given authority to make large decisions. Without good direction, even a company with a history of success or one rich with potential cannot compete, let alone create breakthroughs.

Direction that makes a difference starts with two fundamental assumptions. First, *the chief must manage people, including himself or herself, based on strengths*. Second, *he or she must manage non-strengths*. A one-brainstyle team or department — especially a company — will fall further and further behind. There are too many issues left unaddressed, too little synergy to move forward. This is the <u>true</u> challenge of creating diversity in the workplace: teams of <u>diverse thinkers</u>.

Too often a manager chooses others to work with who have the same brainstyle. That's natural. We like and trust the familiar. But neither a company nor a business center can produce excellence until <u>all</u> brainstyles contribute to outcomes.

Research on high-performing companies by Peter Vaill of George Washington University concludes that to be outstanding a firm needs to operate according to the principle of "joint optimization." Vaill describes this principle as "an organized collection of things and people each operating within its own set of laws, to drive a stream of processes where each element behaves according to its own laws and is not inhibited by any other element."[6] In our words, when each individual is making maximum use of his own brainstyle and not inhibiting any other, you have a high-performing system.

When a team or company breaks free from the limits of one-style management and begins to operate openly from strengths, exciting things begin to happen:

- The right people are in the right jobs. Therefore, they are productive.
- Expectations and promises are openly based on what people

can deliver. Therefore, agreements are kept. Quality is possible.

- The non-strengths of the leader are managed by teamwork. Therefore, the leadership embraces all strengths at all times to address each element of problem-solving.

When all the above are addressed, then consider: Good leadership comes from a blend of natural, **Time Zero** strengths along with those **skills learned from experience.** Knowing how to work with **Time Zero** gives you a place to stand in the present moment. Learned skills, such as knowing what to count on from those in other brainstyles, along with technical and professional background enough to assess and challenge business decisions, (the lessons learned from the resume) give you the strengths necessary to survive any economic stress. But neither will stand alone. Getting the right people in the right jobs has too long been a function of matching your resume with a job description. It is not enough.

To be sure, all kinds of people, people with different brainstyles, end up as chiefs. Some make their way up the ladder one rung at a time; others seem to appear suddenly at the top. Some inherit the job; others are promoted into it. But no matter what route you have followed to get to the top spot, once there, you must employ the **Four Requirements of Leadership** presented below. A team or a company needs a true leader to keep it vital in all economic environments, and each brainstyle requires different kinds of support to pull off the job. For you to be an effective chief, you most likely will have to let go of what you have learned a leader is, and set about honestly assessing what your gifts will produce.

BrainStyle fact #3: *You will lead according to your brainstyle.*

The Four Requirements of Leadership

1. A leader must define the big picture, not the right answer— and get others committed to delivering it. A successful business is powered by a vision for its future that everyone in the team can subscribe to. One of the roles of the leader is to articulate a vision

that takes the group into an unknown future he or she has defined. To do so, a leader must be able to "see" possibilities for the future. If you cannot, you need access to someone who can.

A *leader* is a member of the herd who sees that the direction the herd is heading will take them over the cliff. A leader turns left and gets others to see the wisdom of turning. Others crash into the leader and try to push him or her in the direction they were comfortable heading — over the edge.

As *Inc.* magazine reports on what makes new businesses succeed ("The Truth About Start-Ups"): "Not only can founders foresee *which* challenges will come up, most can practically pinpoint *when*."[7] In order to do this, you must honestly assess the brainstyles of those in your company — the resources you have to anticipate the future.

The popular press has made a "visionary" leader the thing to be — better than being something else. This is too uncomfortable for most, so *leadership* in the popular press is soon defined to include everyone. *Leadership* that is defined so it includes everyone soon becomes a definition that *requires one person to have strengths in all four brainstyle areas*. We expect a leader to be charismatic, visionary, analytical, results-oriented, and sensitive to people. And criticize them when they fail to be them all.

You now know it is impossible to be equally gifted in all areas.

Let us address the underlying issue: one person's strengths do not make them *better*, they make them *different*. It is not better to be able to envision a future ahead of others — it is simply a strength. Having this ability means the person is deficient at other strengths. It is the expectations about leadership that are the real problem.

There is a time to define the overall direction for the future, and then get everyone involved in how to get there. One brainstyle is really gifted at looking over the horizon and creating whole answers. **Conceptors.** And **Conceptors** who focus beyond their own personal interests tend naturally to get others involved in strategizing and making plans workable because those are not their strengths, and they cannot move forward without a tangible, realistic, well-structured plan.

"Leading" to new areas does not require being a **Conceptor,** having a title or status, however. Every other brainstyle takes charge of the area that is their strength, and in which they have developed expertise. They become *idea champions*, standard bearers for excellence, inspirations to us all. They do not reach their goals through *vision* or with the processes of the **Conceptor.** Each moves forward incrementally, and powerfully.

Bob Crandall has created a *direction* for American Airlines: market dominance. He would be the first to say that he did not develop it on his own nor implement it alone. He took on problems methodically, as a **Deliberator** will — thoroughly, step-by-step, driving the systems to execute better and better until the Airline is #1. He is not known as a visionary or a "people person". Does this make him any less successful?

Peter Ueberroth, the **Conciliator** who brought us the spectacularly coordinated 1984 Olympics in Los Angeles achieved outstanding results by putting together a team of professionals who made the event the most spectacular possible. Appearing on television in the '90's, Mr. Ueberroth said his talent is to bring people together to get a job done. He does not say he is a visionary — he doesn't create the Big Picture himself — yet he uses his strengths to *create a direction* — possibilities — to get a world class result.

The **Knower,** Harold Geneen, created one of the largest and most successful businesses — ITT — in a very short space of time with a clear focus on what had to be in place to make the company successful. His "vision" was of flawless systems and well-executed plans that moved the company quickly into market dominance. He used his strengths to hone start-up acquisitions to a fine art.

The **Conceptor** Jack Welch, the leader transforming General Electric for the next century started in the '70's by defining where the business needed to be at the end of the '80's. Naturally, he tells others to be visionaries like him. "Good business leaders create a vision," he states. "They articulate the vision, passionately own the vision and drive it to completion."[8]

We need Welch's vision. His contribution to GE and business in general has been substantial. But Welch is giving <u>his</u> version of a leader. That makes the leader "good." The problem? Having a vision for the business is not *good* or *bad.* It is necessary — and in small doses. Actually, we cannot have all business leaders having *vision* or we would be going in a thousand different directions. *Good* business leaders also *follow* the vision established by Welch, owning the corporate vision and passionately driving their commitment to reach excellence with some learned values. But *each will do this according to his own strengths.*

Given *his* strengths, Welch mandates how to move forward as only a Conceptor might: blending people and business into simple concepts that can be understood and owned by most.

> "For a large organization to be effective, it must be simple. For a large organization to be simple, its people must have self-confidence and intellectual self-assurance. Insecure managers create complexity. Real leaders don't clutter. People must have the self-confidence to be clear, precise, to be sure that every person in their organization — highest to lowest — understands what the business is trying to achieve. But it's not easy. You can't believe how hard it is for people to be simple, how much they fear being simple. They worry that if they're simple, people will think they're simple-minded. In reality, of course, it's just the reverse. Clear, tough-minded people are the most simple."[9]

It must be underscored that being "simple" and "tough-minded" are <u>not</u> everyone's strengths. Creating complexity is not always a result of insecurity. Mr. Welch created a vision, which is his strength. It may not be yours. His definitions help everyone think of *focus, priorities.* Let him and other **Conceptors** contribute this to you or your team. What works for GE or for your own leadership is to *demand excellence from each person's ability to deliver.* Stop asking for "vision" when you really mean excellence in execution. Use "vision" when you need to revitalize, redirect, or invent what's next. And get someone who can really deliver this.

Whether you are a group leader, a supervisor, or a vice president, you can define the gifts you bring to the task and those that others bring. Articulate what is unique about what your team offers. The way you bring your ideas to market as an individual (your brainstyle) will not be unique, but your products and services can be. Success is a synergy of the two. Use brainstyles as a resource to reinvent or drive your unique product or idea.

For a team to inspire and empower their own direction they can create a statement that organization consultant Peter Block calls a *vision of greatness — an expression of the team's values and what they hope to contribute to the organization in the long term.* The process defined by Block in his book *The Empowered Manager*[10] can help people in all organizations build on where they are to get to where they want to go.

The visioning process for you does not have to be an inventive process. It is a discovery process of your personal commitments and values in service of a larger meaning for your life. All brainstyles need to look at what a personal Purpose is — to give scope and meaning to your efforts and put you in a position to be the "maker of your own life."

2. <u>A leader must be able to use conflict to further the business.</u> There is no escaping conflict in business because business is about making decisions about how resources will be used. Deciding for one thing automatically means deciding against all other options. Each option comes with an advocate, and so a leader may spend 90 percent of his time dealing with conflicting allegiances. At the same time, the long-range goals of the company must be kept in clear view. How well do you handle conflict at **Time Zero**? How well do you push ideas that go against the tide of current wisdom and seek to expand the issue for everyone?

A *leader* uses conflict to surface issues, redefine direction, and move the entire organization forward. A *manager* defines and personally helps resolve conflict that ends in *win-win results* for the people involved while supporting the business as a whole. We must have an enormous number of competent managers who can do this.

For most at the supervisory level, handling conflict is a smaller part of the job — the major part is focusing on the work itself. The higher up the ladder you go in business the more conflicts are part of the job. Here is where brainstyle is the critical factor in promotion: **Time Zero** decision-making skills become ever more critical as responsibility increases. Only those who have a realistic appraisal of their ability to respond to conflict will be able to move a team forward at full speed. Those who do not deal well with conflict at **Time Zero** must and will slow things down.

Conciliators and **Deliberators** are wise to learn and practice skills in conflict resolution so that they have a process they can use from memory. Even so, these two brainstyles are best and most natural at summarizing or harmonizing. Both can attack another when angry. But confrontation that involves give and take will always be a stretch. Therefore, more time is needed for reaching an outcome for these brainstyles. **Knowers** need to <u>add</u> time to their natural quick resolution when emotions are involved. **Conceptors** have the brainstyle strengths to deal with both feelings and issues — their approach needs the discipline of focus and the patience to thoroughly address the problems presented.

An ability to question and challenge is at the core of the businesses that Richard Pascale assessed in his study of the ten remaining "excellent" companies (44 were originally listed by Peters and Waterman in *In Search of Excellence*.) He cites Honda as "one of the best-managed companies in the world"[11] because of an ability to have employees mirror the top management in *constructive use of conflict*. Employees "reexamine assumptions and chip away at defect rates, cycle time, and inefficiencies."[12] The basic structure of the business is one which pits experts and business centers against one another. This has made the smaller of Japan's automotive companies the most formidable. Conflict is essential.

The thrust of American training programs is that conflict must be "managed." Conflict is undesirable. Conflict means you have lost control. And losing control is very undesirable in a left brain system. But does any company or team exist strictly in a controlled, measurable, left-brain system? <u>Hardly</u>.

If you are experiencing a great deal of conflict and frustration with others on the job, there are several possible causes:

• You are in the wrong job. There is a conflict between your natural gifts and what you are trying to deliver.

• You are working with others who have *similar* brainstyles and you are focusing on the details, relationships, procedures and activities and losing the focus and satisfaction that larger goals and broader targets bring.

• You are working with *different* brainstyles and expecting to feel personally comfortable rather than professionally challenged.

• You are experiencing the frustrations of working toward a deadline with those whose brainspeeds are different than yours. You do not have a *strength contract* with your peers to establish a process for working together where each can contribute using their own timing.

As soon as there are deadlines, there are conflicts. If we had all the time in the world, we would work things out — eventually. But deadlines demand measures. Measures invoke comparisons. Fast is good. Slow is bad — *unless* we look at how best to get to the deadline with others.

Efforts to transform the cultures of major corporations are focusing on training for teams and project solving groups to unleash "employee creativity."[13] *Better to unleash constructive conflict based on the natural clash of people at their best.* This is the real and necessary diversity. Data on team results which are made up of people who think differently show that once these teams learn how to work together by *using* differences rather than resisting them, solutions reached are far better than with groups of people who think similarly.[14] The efforts of government mandated programs which still insist on diversity of *appearance* do not address the core of the issue.

3. <u>A leader must achieve results through others' strengths</u>. In teams, start-up companies or mega-corporations, delegation is at the core of the business. As *Inc.* reports about those trying to get a business going: "Founders were thrown for a loop by the responsibilities of being CEO...Those who delegated well didn't get overwhelmed by minutiae. Others got buried."[15]

Delegation is at the core of leadership and depends on *The BrainStyles System*™ to work. Only by understanding and exploiting the strengths of other brainstyles can a CEO — or a supervisor — lead a company to success. Where people are concerned, there are always two rules:

> *Rule Number 1: People will never do what you want*
> *them to do. Corollary to Rule Number 1: People will do*
> *things "right" for their <u>own</u> reasons.*

Using brainstyles puts you in a position to ask the right people — teammates, subordinates, or executives — to do what they are going to do in the way they will do it naturally. This is also what they do best. Training requires the entire team or organization to develop expectations of one another based on individual **Time Zero** strengths — *instead of demanding comfort.* This is where the most attention is needed. This is where personal demands are the most extreme. It is <u>not</u> natural to expect another to do things <u>his</u> way. We all must grow to allow others to do things their way. To apply this one simple principle is an act of daily acceptance which will mean personal change for everyone — and lead to enormous success.

4. <u>A leader must anticipate change in a disciplined way.</u> The ability to cope with change is crucial to a good leader. It requires constant **Time Zero** decisions about the *details* with the *vision in full view.* There cannot, on the other hand, be change just for change' sake. As <u>Inc.</u> reports,

What has made or broken many of the companies we've watched, though, is this: the ability (or inability) to recognize and react to the completely unpredictable....To be flexible, and not just in response to small surprises but to really big ones — like discovering you're selling to the wrong customers or selling through an entirely wrong channel.[16]

Disciplined change demands that a leader respond to others both reasonably and imaginatively. The immature **Conceptor** can be a changer. A single-brainstyle team or company has little chance of reacting quickly enough to the demands of the marketplace. Including, developing, and knowing how to use the right-brainstyle of the **Conceptor** and **Conciliator** are vital to meet this criterion. Where consultants demand that individuals learn to be *balanced,* we say *put together a balance in the team.*

To lead, you multiply your reach by starting with your own strengths and then filling in non-strengths to meet the Four Requirements of Leadership. The requirements remain constant; how you fill those requirements depends wholly on your brainstyle.

Experts in corporate culture agree that the character of the team or company can be shaped by the person at the top. In the past that shaping has meant that the company as a whole looks pretty much like its CEO or the team acts like its leader. But just as a pot is shaped by the potter without looking like him, a company or a team can be shaped by leadership without becoming a one-style enterprise unable to manage its non-strengths or too stuck in its sameness to move into the future with breakthroughs in thinking. Preparation starts for the job of CEO from whatever job you are currently holding. It does not include trying to learn to be what your not. If the top spot is not for you, the rules still apply.

What Kind of Leader Are You?
Are you patterning yourself after some role model who you

admire? Do they have your strengths? Or are they someone you *should be*? What kind of leader are you striving to be?

To confront this question objectively is the toughest challenge for the achiever, especially the highly motivated, self starter we all admire. To tell someone who is willing to go all out to get to a goal that they are *limited* — that they must focus a single set of strengths to reach their potential is just unacceptable for many. Yet if you meet the most successful of people, they have come to terms with themselves. And this "coming to terms" means, primarily, an acceptance of their limitations. They know what they can really deliver.

Being a Leader, Being Yourself, Being the Maker of Your Own Life

Anyone can take on the role of "leader" by taking personal responsibility for an area of their life or work.

Bob, a very capable **Deliberator** and very frustrated technician, worked in Quality Control for a manufacturing company. He had several conversations with his boss about leaving the company and returning to school for an advanced degree. He talked about how difficult his job was — continually confronting production supervisors (a non-strength for Bob) about the poor quality of the products they were making. He talked about the leadership needed to produce better products by demanding closer adherence to formulas. When Bob talked about leadership in those days, he meant senior management.

And then several events occurred. Bob attended a class in how to teach quality measurement to everyone in an organization. He got very excited. So excited that he called the company president on a Sunday morning and asked if he could come visit briefly that day. When he arrived he handed the president a thick report. "This is a proposal about Quality. But it's more than that. I'm sick of waiting for <u>you</u> to fix things around here. <u>I</u> am taking responsibility. No more waiting around and feeling frustrated — I am going to personally teach S.P.C. (Statistical Process Control) to everyone in this company. I don't even know how to go about it, but I've got some ideas. Here's my proposal. I want to meet tomorrow to talk about how to start."

Bob, with his technical background, strength in building a consensus, discussing ideas, and following through on a plan, initiated his own step-by-step training process for teams throughout the company. The result was an award to Bob's company as the outstanding quality supplier in its industry, along with an entire company proud of a sizeable achievement.

Working from his strengths, Bob decided to make a difference regardless of his designated authority. Previously seeking more job satisfaction in situations outside his own control, he created his own. He did it from his strengths, by bringing value to others, solving a vital problem and enrolling support — a win-win for everyone.

Applying brainstyles to groups, teams, or organizations means creating cultures that shift the responsibility from "them" to the people who lead and work in them. Using brainstyles means demanding more of what we can really deliver from ourselves. It means there will be an automatic lessening of demand for others to be who they are not. Applying brainstyles to our daily lives means demanding that people start being more themselves and less a "model." There must be room and time for different ways of thinking and processing information, different ways of behaving and speaking about problems.

Accepting who we are and who we are not is the basis for a loving, sane way of living with ourselves and one another.

Appendix A:

BrainStyles Background

APPENDIX A:

BRAINSTYLES BACKGROUND

Where These Ideas Come From. And Where They Don't.

Some 25 centuries ago Hippocrates, in studying the functions of the human body, concluded that there were four fluids (humors) that determined four distinct physical and mental constitutions. His description of what, in the aggregate, was to be called "temperament" and the notion of being in a good or bad "humor" are still with us. With 20th-century technology we are discovering just how the physical brain governs our mental capacities and our behavior — expanding the thesis of the "founder of modern medicine" in the Golden Age of ancient Greece.

How we see ourselves today is greatly influenced by psychologists, who in the 1800's began to study in a disciplined way how and why people act the way they do. Sigmund Freud (1856-1939), the Viennese physician who founded modern psychoanalysis, has been one of the most influential. Freud posited that people are driven by a single, sexual motive. In the first half of the 20th century many psychologists, following Freud, defined human behavior as the end product of trying to satisfy inner "drives." In America, in particular, the notion of a single human dynamic fit in well with the desire for social equality; it tended to show how people are all fundamentally the same.

Carl Jung (1875-1961), a Swiss psychiatrist and the most famous of Freud's students, disagreed. In 1920 he argued that people are different in fundamental ways. "Psychological types," as he defined them, were distinct groups of people with marked differences in behavior, differences logically derived from *observable differences in mental functioning.*

To behaviorists, like the American J.B. Watson and his contemporary the Russian Ivan Pavlov (1849-1936), inner motives were murky and untestable. These theorists wanted to define psychology as a science — make it measurable and quantifiable. Pavlov is famous for his experiment with dogs, in which he rang a bell before feeding them, causing them to salivate. He then demonstrated that merely ringing the bell <u>caused</u> the dogs to salivate, ergo, you can *condition* behavior. Watson published a paper in 1913 that established an important 20th-century view of people: psychology, the science of the mind, he said, became the science of *behavior*. Behavior can be observed and measured. Moreover, behavior can be controlled and changed. Indeed, he stated that there are certain behaviors that are *outside personal control*. You occasionally do things that are simply the result of an external source (a stimulus) and the response merely a reflex that can't be helped. In such cases behavior is automatic, he said. The conclusion? We are products of our environment. Watson's ideas shifted responsibility for actions to the outside world.

This view influenced thinking about how to educate people for the next 80 years: What most people thought about child rearing and social interactions involved applying punishments and rewards in order to *change* behavior. The popular mis-application of the work done by the behaviorist B. F. Skinner (b. 1904), the man who described how rewards and punishment work, concluded that others *make* us mad, happy, etc. Watch any program on television and you will see the behaviorist influence: The villain does something bad (negative stimulus) that *forces* a victim to react (try to punish the bad guy) in order to change his behavior. Eric Berne, a Freudian psychologist, captures this world of punishments and consequences: It is a world in which relationships are played out in three roles: *victim, persecutor,* or *rescuer* — helpless, bad guy, and hero.[1] Because one doesn't deal in this system with internal motivations or the notion of individual responsibility, there is blame (who did this?), punishment (I'll get even), and help (I couldn't have done it without you, your gun, your brains). The role of the person with choices is lost. In the world where there is only behavior controlled by outside events we become helpless victims of relationships in which the *outside* must change so *we* can get better.

Behaviorists, such as Skinner, who rejected any internal

causation for actions were labeled "radical" by most psychologists in the field.[2] Even so, behaviorist solutions to human issues were pervasive. It is quick and simple to deal with others in a measurable, structured way (using punishment and reward systems). You actually see a response.

Much of the business transacted between two people is based only on what is seen and heard, taken at face value. Most interpersonal conflict arises from trying to change what you observe using the behaviorist principles. But this strategy is not nearly as potent in influencing behavior as is simple recognition of what is inside the other person's head.

We Are A Product of What's Inside Us.

In the 1940's a validation and expansion of Jung's work on personality types (which declared the human personality a product of internal states) was undertaken by Isabel Myers and Katherine Briggs. Myers identified sixteen "psychological types" by means of the famous Myers-Briggs Type Indicator (a self-testing questionnaire). In *Gifts Differing*, Myers' final book, published in 1980, she asserted that "the theory is that much seemingly chance variation in human behavior is not due to chance; it is in fact the logical result of a few basic, observable differences in mental functioning. These basic differences concern the way people *prefer* to use their minds...."[3]

Jung and Myers saw humans as autonomous beings making choices (preferences) about the way they fulfilled their potential. As Myers observed:

> The basic type differences *appear* as differences in interest, but the division goes very deep and rests on a **natural tendency** to develop in a particular direction and a natural desire for particular goals. Successful development in the natural direction yields not only effectiveness but emotional satisfaction and stability as well, whereas the

thwarting of the natural development strikes at both ability and happiness.[4]

Jung observed, and Myers substantiated, the role the external environment plays in making us who we are. It can "thwart," but it does not determine. In fact, people who give up their natural *internal* gifts to try to fit someone else's expectations for *external* behavior Jung describes as disempowered "victims." Autonomy and power derive from a full expression of a person's **natural** gifts.

> If the direction of the development were entirely dependent on the environment, there would be nothing to be thwarted, but, in fact, a main hazard to good type development is the opposing pressure of the environment.
> ...when an environment, squarely conflicting with their capacities, forces children to depend on unnatural processes or attitudes, the result is a falsification of type, which robs its victims of their real selves and makes them into inferior, frustrated copies of other people."[5]

Several years ago Dorothy and Robert Bolton, two students of the author and industrial psychologist David Merrill[6], wrote a book called *Social Style/Management Style.*[7] Both authors thoroughly explain and advance Merrill's behavioral social styles system. The focus of Merrill's work, was to track ways of approaching yourself and others by dealing with directly observable behavior. "Social styles" were introduced and defined as ways to recognize and predict peoples' patterns of interpersonal behavior. Merrill developed two critical dimensions of behavior to use in defining a social style: those behaviors which try to control others (degrees of assertiveness) and those behaviors which are attempts to control one's self (degrees of responsiveness or emotionality). Using these criteria, it was explained, you can quickly categorize people into one of four groups with certain predictable behavior patterns.. The Boltons assert:

> "A central theme of the social style concept is: Excel at being what you are, rather than try to be what you are not. Social style teaching does not suggest that you alter the "essential you." It does not attempt to overhaul you so you will fit some supposedly superior style. Indeed, research shows that every style is effective if it is implemented well and is appropriate to the situation."[8]

However, just as importantly, they also present a method for "inter-personal flexibility."[9] The theory they present says: identify another person's style by how much he controls and how strongly he reacts, then "flex" (modify your behavior) to adapt to that person. For example, a person who naturally asks questions and lets others take the lead (acts "less assertively") should, when dealing with someone who is naturally direct, forceful, and decisive ("highly assertive"), look the more assertive person in the eye and be as direct and forceful as he/she is. The Boltons add a very real caution: "As a conscious approach to work relationships, style flex needs to be done only occasionally — at moments when the stakes are important. To flex one's style all the time would be to lose one's sense of self — probably the greatest loss of all."[10]

Perhaps you <u>can</u> learn to "flex" temporarily in important situations and still avoid losing your sense of self. A real value can be brought to relationships where someone is trying to meet another's needs. We say the focus will not work in the long run. The focus on behavior will lead you astray.

Attempting to identify who a person truly is by observing his behavior can be very complicated and misleading. Merrill's social styles model explains the complexity of behaviors that people exhibit by identifying people as combinations of styles. This complexity confuses and complicates. There is no clear base from which to work. Even Jung says trying to develop all four "processes," as he called them, promotes immaturity.[11] People learn how to handle different situations with different skills and can *appear* to operate with a brainstyle other than their own. Just don't be deceived. If you look closely, these individuals do not perform any activity outside their own brainstyle with the same skill as they do those with their natural brainstyle. And they never do in a new situation where there is no stored memory or previous learned experience. All the work they are encouraged to do to adapt is ultimately demoralizing.

Caution: Watch out for a behavioral approach in popular seminars and books that offers a superficial approach to life — fix the behavior and fake the result. When you try to modify your behavior to match another "style" — even on a temporary basis — you create the expectation that you will also *perform* like them. The bottom-line of brainstyles is to negotiate how to <u>work</u> together, not to make one another comfortable. The focus in brainstyles is on mastering your strengths and living from them honestly. Adapting your gifts to be somehow different can only be useful in the short term, if that. As you already know, behavior modification is a temporary solution. *Science News* reported a study conducted with 46 couples in marriage counseling over 20 years.[12] The couples who participated in *behavioral* counseling for marital problems (they changed things they did and said with one another) had a significantly higher divorce rate (19 of 23) than couples participating in "insight therapy". The latter helps individuals resolve past emotional issues (previous decisions) that block communication and has much longer lasting effects, promoting autonomy for each person. (Only 1 of 23 couples divorced after this type of therapy.) Similarly, our brainstyles system demands that you look beneath the surface, and not simply adjust behaviors for a temporary "fix." The application of ideas will pay off in self-awareness and working relationships that are satisfying rather than merely compromises.

Environmental Influences

A study on Kauai, Hawaii of 698 "high-risk children" over a 32-year period finds that successful characteristics that carried people through "the most discordant and impoverished homes, beset by physical handicaps" were present in the children as infants, and were well established by the age of <u>one</u>. Two out of three children developed serious learning or behavior problems by the age of ten. "Surprisingly, however, one out of every three of them...developed instead into competent, confident, and caring young adults." The environment (parenting, material advantages, etc.,) was <u>not</u> the determining factor. All grew up in an equally stressful and impoverished environment.[13]

What these children were exhibiting was a <u>genetic</u> characteristic that has been measured for the first time by a researcher who studied twins. The president of the Society for Psychophysiological Research, David Lykken, presented a paper in 1981 in which he announced some remarkable new findings about heredity. His hypothesis is called "*emergenesis*" and has been statistically verified over and over again. Basically, "emergenic" characteristics are those that are genetically based, deriving from a synergy of genetic materials in an individual, but <u>not</u> <u>directly</u> <u>passed</u> <u>on</u> <u>from</u> <u>the</u> <u>parents</u>. Lykken's study has enormous implications for how we consider what we inherit and therefore can't change. For instance, he showed that certain twins born from the same egg (monozygotic), whether raised together or apart, "indicate a significant genetic influence" for "<u>positive</u> <u>affect</u>." Never before have we considered attitudes part of our genetic makeup.[14]

A number of studies of biological twins, done in an intensive and exhaustive way, have produced ground-breaking results. Starting in 1970, Dr. Lykken, working at the University of Minnesota, and others interviewed and extensively tested same-egg (identical) twins raised apart, comparing them with other identical twins raised together, non-identical twins (dizygotic), and cousins. In 1981 he reported a "surprisingly strong (70 - 80%) influence of <u>genetic</u> variation on aptitudes, psychophysiological characteristics,

personality traits and even dimensions of attitude and interest."
What was found, to simplify the story enormously, was that genetic
makeup can account for statistically valid predictable features,
such as *intelligence* — how many answers and how fast they are
answered, *brain activity* measured by an EEG
(electroencephalograph), even *skin response* — all measurable,
testable. Positive correlations abounded to show that same-egg
twins who had been separated at birth evinced strikingly similar
behaviors. In fact, a questionnaire that measured *conservatism*
showed a genetic basis!

> One might be inclined to doubt that Conservatism —
> the tendency to endorse conservative traditional
> values — has any genetic basis at all. The fact that
> this trait correlates .74 in our sample of MZA twins
> [identical twins from the same egg, raised apart],
> however, suggests that the genetic influence actually
> is considerable; perhaps William Buckley Jr. and I.F.
> Stone, Jr. owe their positions on the political
> spectrum as much to their genomes as to the
> example set by their parents.

Likewise, Lykken was able to establish a genetic basis for *how
outgoing a person is:*

> "Social Potency...measures the self-perceived ability
> to influence, lead, or dominate others and the
> amount of social impact one has...Our MZA twins
> correlate .67 on Social Potency and the 247 pairs of
> MZT twins [identical twins raised together] are
> correlated .65. The 122 sets of DZ [fraternal] twins,
> however, correlate .07, nearly zero."[15]

The only reason that the MZ (identical) twins could score the
way they did would be their genetic similarity.

Lykken's proof for "emergenesis" which radically revises how we separate what we can learn from what our genetic makeup prescribes is a complex idea. It is the basis for saying that we are both limited and unlimited at the same time. How our individual genetic material comes together is, as the geneticists say, the cards we are dealt at birth. He gives a striking example:

> I think some form of emergenesis must be invoked to explain how the union of a bricklayer and a peasant woman produced a Karl Frederich Gauss and also why Gauss's offspring showed virtually none of his mathematical talent (one son could do extensive arithmetic computations in his head but this was at best just a facet of the genius that made his father `the prince of mathematicians'.)[16]

Lykken's work has been cited again and again as some of the strongest evidence of a genetic basis for who we become and against the power of the environment, including parenting and heritage, to determine who we turn out to be. It also is an extraordinary breakthrough in our thinking about our own limitations.

Two child psychologists at Pennsylvania State University take up the application of genetics in their studies of children and their families with a focus on siblings. Robert Plomin and Judy Dunn talk about the effect of the family on the young child:

> 'It's startling at first,' Plomin admits. `But all the evidence points to the same conclusion: What we've thought of all along as `shared family environment' doesn't exist.' That's because we each carry around between our ears our own little customized version of our environment. From our first days of life, and perhaps even before, we perceive everything that

happens to us through a unique filter, every skewed event changing us in a way that affects how we'll experience the next event.

What you do to and for your offspring matters very much, *but only in ways you can't control or even foresee.* The filter through which your child perceives you and the world is constantly evolving, and is partly of his or her own making.

Dunn, who observes children for a living, thinks parents should take away a different, more comforting message. I'd say, 'Relax,' she says. 'I'm constantly struck by the power of children's personalities, almost irrespective of what their parents do.'[17]

Accepting Our Limits Means We Can Be Unlimited.

We are *not* simply a product of our environment and how we are reared. We *are* limited by the "cards we were dealt." And each of us has a need to express an inner potential.

There now exists the technology to explain and simplify the basic differences in "mental functioning" in people — a roadmap for how we organize and express who we are. We now know that the mental preferences Jung and Myers spoke of do <u>not</u> include choosing *a way to think*, but just as vast a territory: how to <u>expand</u> the genetic gifts or mental "hardware" we were born with. As we accept that we have certain capabilities and not others, we find a simple way to build the foundation of a strong self-esteem. In assuming the responsibility for these gifts, we take charge of our autonomy and get out of the victim-persecutor-rescuer loop that Berne described. We can learn how to look past behavior to the strengths underneath. And with this perspective, we can direct our abilities to solving problems that can be solved, while letting go of others that we have no chance of influencing — like the way other people think and behave. Who we are is up to each one of us.

The Brain

In 1981, psychobiologist Roger Sperry won the Nobel Prize for Physiology and Medicine for his work at the California Institute of Technology on "split-brain" studies on the functions of the two hemispheres of the brain. Sperry, together with a student of his and a neurosurgeon, studied the effects of cutting the *corpus callosum* — the mass of nerve fibers that connects the two hemispheres of the brain — in several people. What Sperry discovered is now commonly known as left-brain right-brain theory. He found that the *corpus callosum* is a communications network that sends information back and forth between the two hemispheres of the brain. Without the link, neither side knew what the other was doing. Moreover, with each hemisphere isolated, Sperry and his associates were able to determine that each hemisphere has distinctly different functions and processes information in its own distinct way. Subsequent tests have documented that in a normally functioning brain the *corpus callosum* enables both hemispheres to work together for almost every activity, although (as they found) one hemisphere or the other will predominate for a specific task. (See pg. 13 for a list of left and right hemisphere functions.)

Since this initial work done by Sperry and his colleagues, much more sophisticated work has been done to show that the "left brain" functions Sperry originally defined as physically based in the left side of the brain are not, in fact, 100% exclusive to the left hemisphere. The same goes for the right side. And communication between these functions is dominated by but not limited to the corpus callosum. Chemicals are released to activate different brain areas in time. This book is using "left-brain" and "right-brain" *as metaphors* for the very complex interactions within the brain of the parts that perform the functions noted as "left" and "right".[18] What is important is that parts of our brain need to communicate with one another in order for us to perform. And that takes *time*.

Robert Ornstein explains it this way:

> We can never operate with a 'full deck' but with only
> a small selection of the total mental apparatus at any
> one time. This means that all our faculties of mind
> are never available at once. So, at any one time we
> are much more limited, much more changeable, than
> we might otherwise believe of ourselves.[19]

We all have access to both sets of functions in both hemispheres, the genetic functions that we were born with. An equally important point is that *we do not access all functions of the brain equally, at the same time, or at the same speed.* As Lykken has shown, in this respect as in others, our hardware uniquely determines how we behave. And, we add, at what speed.

Dr. Terry Brandt, the director of the Center for Staff Development in Houston, works with neurophysiologists and other specialists to track how the brain works to solve problems. One of his findings is the measurement of the neuron firings generated by the brain when we think. He reports that the number of "thoughts" (information bits) registered inside the human brain is about 50,000 per minute. This *exceeds by hundreds of times* the number of sensory inputs we register. We can literally measure the fact that we generate more "thoughts" inside our own brain than we get input from the environment. The conclusion: *we* sort through and choose what we get from the environment, selectively. This is obvious every day: people hear what they want to hear, see what they want to see, and report different interpretations of the same event.

As one of the neurophysiologists who Dr. Brandt works with put it on measuring how the brain works, "you create your own reality."

Beyond this, Dr. Brandt reports, "we have enough genetic material to account for about 100,000 connections in the brain; however, the potential for the number of connections is approximately 10^{15} (a *quadrillion*). The difference is a combination of us acting upon the environment and the environment acting on us."[20] We literally expand our own intelligence by many magnitudes as we process information about, and react to, the environment.

Doesn't it make sense that using our *natural* capacities will lead to greater results?

In *Frames of Mind, The Theory of Multiple Intelligences*,[21] a book by psychologist and MacArthur Prize Fellow Howard Gardner, he proposes that "intelligence" is the ability to solve problems or create products — not at all what is measured by an IQ test. He proposes seven kinds of intelligence, including the [right-brain] body control displayed by athletes and dancers, musical talent, and interpersonal skills, such as being able to read another's feelings. Standard IQ testing is based on the premise that all brains work alike and all have a general set of skills. Not so. Seymour Epstein, a psychologist at the University of Massachusetts, says "IQ and success in living have little to do with each other." Looking at new ways to determine success in life defines a different kind of intelligence critical for success: emotional intelligence. Psychologist Robert Sternberg at Yale is studying what makes people succeed in life. The three criteria for success in business written about in the book *Practical Intelligence*,[22] with Dr. Wagner are directly addressed by *The BrainStyles System*™. They are: *how well a person manages himself* (understands his own strengths and non-strengths), *how well a person manages others* by knowing their strengths and non-strengths, and finally, *how well a person manages one's own career*. The executives who scored the best on a test devised by the authors and based on their book tended to have more years of management experience and to be better paid than those who did less well.

The Brain and BrainStyles

Different basic brain processing produces different types of abilities or strengths. What we recognize as "intelligence" is largely a product of brain <u>speed</u> — or how fast a processor one is in moving back and forth in the brain's functions and retrieving from memory.

Hans J. Eysenck, a British neurological researcher, has proven that the genetically determined speed and efficiency of brain processing correlates directly with "intelligence" measured on intelligence tests. Eysenck, followed by those studying artificial intelligence with computers, are exploring the beginning of what brainstyle theory proposes: genetics (with a factor of 80% to 90%) determine brain make-up and speed (the hardware). Brain speed is responsible for communication between parts of the brain itself, and is the critical factor in determining strengths. This communication between parts of the brain we call *brainstyle.* It also defines how memories are stored. As Gary Lynch, psychobiologist at the University of California at Irvine says, "Once a pattern is formed [for memory], the pathways are there forever."[23] So as we acquire memories, we lay down neural pathways that help us organize what we see. We add infinite numbers of them. We imprint our memories through our brainstyle — processing of information, which in turn determines what we perceive and "know." *Brainstyle* and "intelligence" are distinct concepts. As psychologists are finding, the notion of intelligence has been extremely narrow. Recent work proposes considering the intelligence of different strengths. This is how, then, we can unlock the potential of future generations, assessing intelligence by different brainstyles, and giving up the idea of <u>one</u> model.

Ned Herrmann, president of Applied Creative Services, Ltd., in North Carolina, is a pioneer in the field of identifying how "four quadrants" in the brain (the left and right brain discussed in upper and lower halves) specialize in abilities that become patterns of behavior. Much of his work is directed at helping people discover differences between left- and right-brain thinking as well as the subtleties of what different brain patterns dictate in people's preferences. Herrmann has developed a seminar designed to enhance creativity based on his brain research. He reinforces the notion that our brain is part of our hardware. "In my view, brain dominance is part of the 'human condition'. We are handed, footed, eyed and brained."[24] Herrmann talks about how brain hemisphere specialization by one of four sections of the brain results in people choosing "occupations that offer an opportunity for that person to perform in his or her area of mental preference, thus providing the opportunity to be 'smart'". We would say that this is the use of a natural strength or brainstyle.

Yet Herrmann uses his insights into how the brain functions to help people *change* and be more *creative.* He believes that people do not use their "whole brain" because they are *afraid* to do so. He encourages people to try creative play, instruction and personal affirmations to "move from the left to the right" brain. To move into a more left-brain mode, he acknowledges, takes "discipline." He asks people to use all four "quadrants" of their brain to engage in "creative tasks that have an applied outcome."

> "If any one of the quadrants is unavailable, then the process tends to either fall apart or be greatly sub-optimized. If, for example, someone denies their feelings, then that kind of physiological feedback is unavailable to give them the needed affirmation that they are on the right track. The individual who simply refuses to engage in any kind of logical processing or rational analysis loses the value of that needed activity when an idea needs to be thought through in terms of its elements as contrasted with the whole. The individual who has never been able to visualize or who feels that fantasy is childish and inefficient denies him- or herself the kind of mental usefulness that Einstein rated at the top of his list of mental priorities. The person who is so utterly bored with any form of structure or detail loses the opportunity to think through a plan of action that would facilitate the problem's solution. So each of these different modes of thinking, which are characteristic of the four quadrants, becomes essential to carrying through the whole process."[25]

Perhaps Herrmann, like others teaching creativity, is merely trying to teach *new attitudes* or *values* (decisions) which can indeed be made anew. However, the strongest message once again, seems to return to the theme of you-can-be-<u>all</u>-things-if-you-try-hard-enough. What if an individual is naturally — genetically — predisposed to processing one kind of information better than another? Why not develop *that* strength? We know, and Herrmann substantiates, that we use different parts of the brain for different tasks. It is an error to once again ask us to be good at everything — using all parts of our brains to get the "whole process." We need to <u>honor</u> our <u>strengths</u>: have fun, play, build self image based on *who we are* — and *ask others to contribute to us* in our areas of non-strengths. It must be okay to be limited. Out of limits come limitless possibilities.

Appendix B:

The BrainStyles Inventory

This Inventory was designed and tested by Marlane Miller and Dr. Lawrence H. Peters of the M.J. Neeley School of Business at Texas Christian University, Fort Worth, Texas.

INTRODUCTION:
THE BRAINSTYLE INVENTORY
AND HOW TO USE IT

The BrainStyle Inventory is not like other "tests" you've taken. It was designed to help you identify your unique *brainstyle.* In reading the book this far, you are learning how to distinguish between your *brainstyle* response to *unfamiliar situations which require you to process or think through information* vs. situations you solve by *recalling or remembering.* In taking this inventory, you may realize that questions that ask you to think of your response to unfamiliar situations (**Time Zero** events) are difficult to separate from those where you may be using experience or memory.

Brainstyle is difficult to recognize because of our ability to remember rapidly. In a new situation we can recall so quickly, it is hard to tell what is memory and what is our actual thinking process. In addition, all of us have had a great deal of experience in reacting to many new or different situations. We have learned that in certain situations, we *should respond* in a certain way — different from the way we naturally respond. We have jobs that put pressure on us to behave in certain ways — ways that are inconsistent with who we really are. In addition, all of us have an image of ourselves which we want others to see. Many times our ideal self-image reflects what we judge as our deficiencies — things we want to change, be better at or admired for, but which are not our natural gifts.

When presented with a **Time Zero** event, you have no choice but to behave in a way that is natural for you. Prior learning, job demands and self-image have little, if any, effect on how we respond in **Time Zero** situations. The problem is that by the time we are adults, there are fewer and fewer completely novel situations for us to face. As a result, it is not easy for us to identify our brainstyle by looking only at our response in new situations.

Brainstyle always shows up as a pattern of strengths over time. You will be most comfortable over the long-term when responding in ways that are based on your brainstyle. You will also be most natural and add your <u>best</u> work with the <u>least</u> effort. When we behave in ways that are inconsistent with our brainstyle, we know it. We must strain to learn. We are anxious, tense, careful, and generally must concentrate all the time if we are going to adapt in this way. When we behave in ways that are consistent with our brainstyle, we simply do what comes naturally, effortlessly—without forced concentration.

When completing The BrainStyle Inventory try to distinguish:
- between what you have learned, or remember, and *what comes naturally*
- between what situations demand of you and *what you are most gifted at doing*
- between how you want to be seen and *how you really are*

About 90 percent of those who use the Inventory are content with the match between the identified brainstyle and its description and their own self-described strengths. If you have questions after taking the Inventory, there is a followup section which attempts to answer them.

The BrainStyle Inventory

This inventory is designed to help you identify your unique brainstyle. The difference between a *brainstyle* and *what we have <u>learned</u> to do* usually shows up in what we tend to do first, or most naturally, in new situations. This becomes a pattern over a period of time as the way we handle many situations best. As you select answers, try to distinguish (1) between what you have learned or remember from what comes naturally, (2) between what situations demand of you and what is most comfortable all the time, and (3) between how you want to be seen and how you really are.

There is no one best brainstyle — therefore, **there are no right or wrong answers to the items on this inventory.** *To identify your unique brainstyle, respond honestly to each item.*

> This inventory has 24 pairs of statements. For each pair, choose the alternative (*"a"* or *"b"*) that best describes you. Use the following scale.
> **A** = ... if **"a"** is **more descriptive** of you than "b"
> **B** = ... if **"b"** is **more descriptive** of you than "a"
> **N** = ... if **neither** statement is descriptive of you

In the example below, many people are aware of having <u>both</u> reactions to different situations. What is significant is which comes <u>first</u> or most naturally — especially in an unfamiliar situation <u>before</u> we draw on what we might have learned to do. If neither sounds like your natural reaction, choose "N" as the alternative for that pair.

<u>SAMPLE ITEM:</u>

> *Put an X for each pair of items ON THE ANSWER SHEET.*

a. *Initially, I tend to react logically in new situations.*
b. *Initially, I tend to react intuitively in new situations.*

<u>ANSWER</u> <u>SHEET</u>:   __X__ A   ___ B ___ N

> *This person marked "A" on the answer sheet meaning that the first statement, A, is most descriptive of her natural response in new situations. <u>B</u> <u>is</u> <u>not</u> <u>true</u> <u>until</u> <u>later,</u> or <u>only</u> <u>sometimes</u>.*

 **The BrainStyle Inventory: <u>Scoring Sheet</u>**

Record your responses from *The BrainStyle Inventory* on this sheet. For each item, put an X in the space next to your choice (**A, B, or N**). When you have completed all 24 items, count the number of X's you made in each column and record this number at the bottom of the page.

	1	2	3	4	N
1.	___A			___B	___N
2.		___A	___B		___N
3.	___A	___B			___N
4.	___B			___A	___N
5.	___A		___B		___N
6.	___B		___A		___N
7.			___B	___A	___N
8.	___A			___B	___N
9.		___A		___B	___N
10.	___A	___B			___N
11.	___A		___B		___N
12.		___A	___B		___N
13.			___A	___B	___N
14.	___B	___A			___N
15.		___A	___B		___N
16.			___A	___B	___N
17.	___A	___B			___N
18.	___A			___B	___N
19.		___A		___B	___N
20.		___A	___B		___N
21.		___A		___B	___N
22.	___A		___B		___N
23.			___A	___B	___N
24.		___B		___A	___N

Totals:

<u>Col 1</u>	<u>Col 2</u>	<u>Col 3</u>	<u>Col 4</u>	<u>N</u>
___	___	___	___	

The column with the largest total score should reflect your unique brainstyle. Compare this result with the brief description that follows to see if it describes your strengths.

> **A** = **"a"** *is* **more descriptive** *than b*
> **B** = **"b"** *is* **more descriptive** *than a*
> **N** = **neither** *statement is descriptive*

SECTION I

1a. In new situations, I often have no reaction until I think things over. I am aware of my analysis before I am aware of my feelings.

1b. In new situations, I have spontaneous reactions that I often share with others quickly. I am aware of my feelings before I am aware of my analysis.

2a. My decisions are a result of good logic — I'm not easily swayed off a logical alternative by feelings or intuition.

2b. My decisions are a result of intuition as much as analysis, based on an early, global understanding of the issue. I can easily re-invent the decision to go in a whole new direction if needed.

3a. Typically, I do <u>not</u> make a decision quickly in new areas. I remain tentative in order to assess more information regardless of my feelings.

3b. Typically, I make up my mind quickly in new areas and seldom reconsider whether my decisions were right.

4a. I am best at open-ended brainstorming with others.

4b. I am best where factual information and thorough analysis are the main focus.

5a. Although I can set a direction when given a new problem to solve, **I am best** at working out and refining a plan to solve it, including the necessary details.

5b. When given a new problem to solve, **I am best** at creating a *new* direction and not as good at specifying or following through with the details.

> **A** = "a" is more descriptive *than b*
> **B** = "b" is more descriptive *than a*
> **N** = **neither** *statement is descriptive*

6a. I'm **best** in situations that require **inventing** new solutions over those that rely upon previous experience.

6b. I'm **best** in situations where I can draw on what I already know and can recall from **experience.**

7a. I am naturally friendly. A pattern of mine is to spend more time building relationships than on developing ideas.

7b. I am naturally inventive. A pattern of mine is to spend more time on developing ideas than on building relationships.

8a. In a <u>new</u> situation, I naturally focus on the **facts and details first.** Only later do I understand how I feel about them.

8b. In a <u>new</u> situation, my first reactions are **feelings about the facts or details.** Only later do I become more objective or neutral about them.

9a. I am better at developing practical solutions than in developing people. I'm better at figuring out what needs to get done than in getting others to do it.

9b. I am better at making solutions apply to people, even though I can also develop solutions. I'm best as part of a team or when I'm including and developing others.

10a. I am naturally thorough. I can stay objective for an extended time while collecting information.

10b. I am naturally efficient. I reach a conclusion early on and don't mind taking a stand based purely on my judgments.

> **A** = **"a"** *is* **more descriptive** *than b*
> **B** = **"b"** *is* **more descriptive** *than a*
> **N** = **neither** *statement is descriptive*

11a. Of all the things I do with a <u>new</u> problem, I contribute most by **using a methodical process to compare it** to a **previous** situation and then **assess what might go wrong** in the future.

11b. Of all the things I do with a <u>new</u> problem, I contribute most when I **establish** the **concept** or **overview** that leads to new, stand-alone solutions.

12a. When I deal with an unfamiliar problem, I typically come up with new ways to **apply existing ideas** to solve it which are **practical** and **make immediate sense.**

12b. When I deal with an unfamiliar problem, I typically use contradictory information to **go beyond existing ideas** and **provide a general direction** on how to solve it.

13a. Of all the aspects of problem-solving, I am the best at **inventing** new, unheard-of, **long-term strategies and directions.**

13b. Of all the aspects of problem-solving, I am best at **solving existing** *people* problems with imaginative alternatives or ways to get to a goal.

14a. I'm best at immediately defining the one best answer to solve a problem. I only focus on the highest priorities while working on the solution to ensure the problem gets fixed.

14b. I'm best at immediately assessing a problem against previous criteria to see what's wrong now. I have many priorities while working on the solution to ensure the work gets done correctly.

> **A** = **"a"** *is* **more descriptive** *than b*
> **B** = **"b"** *is* **more descriptive** *than a*
> **N** = **neither** *statement is descriptive*

15a.I am best at creativity sessions where I can brainstorm practical, new applications for existing ideas and state them clearly for others.

15b.I am best at creativity sessions where ideas do not have to make sense or apply immediately. My strength is in dealing with ambiguity and making it apply to real problems. Others can have a hard time understanding me at first.

16a.Initially, my new ideas are often unusual or conceptual enough that there is no consensus or even a majority of support. I can still push a new direction.

16b.Initially, I want a consensus where everyone feels good about my idea. I get personally invested in issues often, even though I try not to.

17a.I first assess new situations, breaking them down into pieces for further study. I react personally sometime later.

17b.I form quick solutions to new situations. It's typically all that's needed. I rarely react personally.

18a.I immediately **analyze** and **evaluate** ideas and feelings, and as a result, I am best at adding more rational solutions based on my expertise.

18b.I **react spontaneously** to people's immediate feelings or the group's dynamics, and as a result, am best at adding solutions based on my sensitivity to others.

19a.I naturally attend **more to the facts** than my feelings or reactions in a situation, even though I have learned to attend to both.

19b.I naturally attend more to **my reactions or feelings about the facts** in a situation, although I have learned to attend to both.

A =	**"a"** *is* **more descriptive** *than b*
B =	**"b"** *is* **more descriptive** *than a*
N =	**neither** *statement is descriptive*

20a. When a **new** problem is presented, I make a simple, fast, factual analysis that is clear and to the point and can solve the problem as stated.

20b. When a **new** problem is presented, I often pose contradictory trial solutions that define the concept or long range direction for the entire problem.

21a. I am often abrupt and concise because I rarely personalize things. I just want to get to the bottom line as quickly as I can.

21b. I take time because I *feel* others' feelings. I often personalize things, so I often try for agreement where everyone feels good about me as well as the idea.

22a. When presented an opportunity, I first carefully get all the facts and look for what could go wrong in order to evaluate it against previous experience.

22b. When presented an opportunity, I first envision total success before considering the negatives. I do not consider previous experience until <u>later</u>.

23a. I am at my best **inventing whole strategies and long term directions for unfamiliar projects** which include others in discussions all along the way.

23b. I am at my best **getting other people excited** about a long term direction I support **after** it has been defined.

24a. Overall, **intuition and feeling come first** and play a larger part than logic and practicality in my decisions.

24b. Overall, **logic and practicality come first** and play a larger part than feelings in my decisions.

BrainStyles Descriptions

If your highest score was COLUMN 1

The DELIBERATOR

> *A person who brings Reason*
> memory first then left or right brain processes; wants to understand first; asks why; assesses what exists; looks for "gaps" or "what's wrong"; focuses on what's rational; analytical; establishes or applies rules; likes precedents; evaluates new directions; innovates; discourages or avoids conflict.

If your highest score was COLUMN 2

The KNOWER

> *A person who brings Clarity*
> left brain first, right brain delayed; responds with conclusions first, then gets facts or has feelings later; strong on deciding answers, planning, organizing; direct, often domineering; practical, innovative with existing ideas; focuses on results, goals, specific tasks; comfortable with confrontation; often invites it.

If your highest score was COLUMN 3

The CONCEPTOR

> *A person who brings Vision*
> left-right brain exchange; generalizes first; gives or needs overview; original; makes up new rules; likes change; prefers concepts; envisions without precedent; focuses on new ideas, possibilities; often criticized for being unrealistic; dislikes details, procedures, follow through; sees conflict as necessary to solve problems.

If your highest score was COLUMN 4

The CONCILIATOR

> *A person who brings Meaning*
> right brain first, left brain delayed; responds or feels first then examines facts and issues; spontaneous reactions to new ideas; often changes mind upon reflection, but can be stubborn; focuses on relationships; intuitive; reads people well; empathizes; imaginative risk taker; hates conflict; tries to foster consensus.

If You Have Questions After Taking the Inventory. . .

Q. What if the brainstyle description I scored highest in doesn't seem to fit?

About 90% of those who use the inventory the first time are content with the match between their score to determine *brainstyle,* the description of the brainstyle strengths, and their own self-described strengths. If you find that you disagree with the brainstyle identified, or have equal scores for two or more brainstyle categories, you are probably focusing too much on prior learning, job demands or self-image. Use the score sheet to go back to the items that compare the two brainstyles you are considering. Go back through the items and ask yourself, "Which response is most natural for me — effortless to do, and which I have a pattern of doing in a variety of situations?" "In new and unfamiliar situations, which do I do first? Which is true of me in new situations in general?"

It is not uncommon for many of the 10 percent who are not content with their first score, or those with a tied score, to change their responses to one that they eventually find to fit. It just might take you some more time to identify your brainstyle. You may need to read more or discuss your profile with someone else you knows you well and understands *brainstyles.*

Here are some of the comments of the those who reconsidered their first responses:

> Mary:
> "I see now that I would *think ahead* about the issues to be dealt with in a meeting, so that when I got there, I was more decisisve and faster than others. These were <u>not</u> **Time Zero's** for me. That's why I answered questions about making fast decisions the way I did originally."
>
> Mary originally scored as a **Knower,** learned more

about **Time Zero**, thought it over and re-scored as a **Deliberator.**

Barry:
"When I filled it out, I thought of times where I'm very intuitive and know my feelings. After thinking about it, I know I first <u>assess</u> — both feelings <u>and</u> facts, but don't make a decision until <u>later</u>. The truth seems to be that I have learned to handle a lot of situations, so that I am now comfortable enough with my early assessment to quickly be aware of my gut feelings, or alternatives about a situation. But first comes the analysis, <u>then</u> the intuition."

Barry had even scores for both **Conciliator** *and* **Deliberator,** re-examined questions and scored as a **Deliberator.**

Mark:
"I was confused. I know I'm impatient and often abrupt. I react quickly to issues. I guess after thinking about it for awhile, I first react a lot with feelings and do take things personally, which is why I now realize I have a feeling-first brainstyle. I thought I acted with no feelings — and I do. But *first* I'm a very emotional guy."

Mark originally assessed himself as a **Knower,** then rescored as a **Conciliator.**

Jim:
"After talking it over, I see I am very fast in areas I

already know about — so when I think about the job, I think of these areas. That's why I answered many questions as a rapid decision-maker. But overall, I really am not, I assess things more thoroughly and don't jump to conclusions — especially on new things."

Jim originally scored as a **Knower,** then rescored as a **Deliberator.**

Some other questions raised by *The BrainStyle Inventory* are:

Q. When I took the inventory, I got to thinking about situations I've learned to handle, and how I often see the big picture in those. I project into the future and set up long range goals. It seems natural to me. Is this part of my brainstyle?

A. Every brainstyle develops expertise in the areas they choose to master. That expertise (stored information in memory) can be used rapidly, and used as a basis for projecting the future. But each brainstyle will do so using their unique approach to reach a conclusion. This does not mean that the real strength of the brainstyle is to come up with a future scenario in a *new*, or **Time Zero** situation.

Q. My job requires a great deal of analysis and detail. People tell me that I'm very spontaneous and friendly, and I know I am a very feeling person. I don't know how to choose between some of the analytical choices vs. the more feeling or intuitive choices.

A. Many people have this question. The first difficulty in taking *The BrainStyle Inventory* is to think of **Time Zero** situations — and for many, this does not happen very often on your job. Separating yourself from your job setting may be the way to look at your **Time Zero** reactions. Equal scores in more than one *brainstyle* may indicate you're adapting to the setting more than using your natural strengths.

Using The BrainStyle Inventory as a learning tool is very appropriate. The questions may be useful in helping you become more aware of the difference between **Time Zero** situations and those you handle with experience. One thing seems to be true for almost everyone: When you get comfortable with your strengths, you won't want to be different than who you really are.

NOTES/REFERENCES

SECTION

NOTES/REFERENCES

PREFACE

1. Robert Bolton and Dorothy Grover Bolton, *Social Style/Management Style*, (Amacom, 1984), p. 24.

2. Foundation for Inner Peace, (Coleman Graphics, Farmingdale, NY, 1975.)

CHAPTER ONE
It Works To Be Who You Are

1. Warren Bennis, *On Becoming A Leader*, (Addison Wesley, 1989), p. 51.

2. *Fortune*, "BrainPower" June, 1991, pp. 44-60.

3. The Myers-Briggs Type Indicator, Palo Alto, California (Consulting Psychologists Press, 1962).

4. Reported in *USA Today* 2/11/92

5. Reported on National Public Radio, 2/14/92

6. *The Wall Street Journal* 2/6/92

7. Robert Ornstein, *Multimind*, (Doubleday, 1986), p. 36.

8. Ibid., see Chapter 5, "Mind on Brain" pp. 47-66.

9. Ibid., pp. 52-53.

CHAPTER TWO
What Knowing About BrainStyle Can Mean For You

1. Michael Meyer, *The Alexander Complex, The Dreams That Drive The Great Businessmen*, (Times Books, 1989).

2. <u>Ibid</u>., p. 17.

3. David T. Lykken, University of Minnesota, Presidential Address to the Society of Psychophysiological Research, 1981, "Research With Twins: The Concept of Emergenesis," p. 371.

4. In 1989, 180 executives and employees in three southwestern construction firms along with 70 university students were administered a pilot instrument to assess four "decision-styles" modeled on brainstyles theory. This assessment was conducted by H. Thomas Hurt, Ph. D., Professor of Communication Studies of the University of North Texas. In Professor Hurt's study to assess brainstyles, the population he tested was predictive in the variable for gender. Eighty-three percent of the female population were classified as **Conciliators.** The male sample did not classify in any one brainstyle. These numbers reflect a more skewed distribution of women in this brainstyle than our larger sample of 500 business people. These numbers still cannot generalize for all women, in the authors' view.

5. Anne Moir, *Brain Sex: The Real Difference Between Men and Women*, (Lyle Stuart, 1991), as quoted in *USA Today*, July 8, 1991.

6. Dr. Doreen Kimura, "Male Brain, Female Brain: The Hidden Difference," *Psychology Today*, November, 1985, pp. 50-58.

7. Dr. Doreen Kimura, "Profile: Vive La Difference," *Scientific American,* October 1990, p. 42.

8. As reported by James Thornton in "His Brain Is Different," *Self Magazine*, March, 1992, pp. 115-165.

9. Joe Tanenbaum, *Male and Female Realities: Understanding The Opposite Sex,* (R. Erdman, 1991).

10. D. Tannen Ph.D., *You Just Don't Understand,* (Ballantine Books, 1990).

11. As quoted in the article "Sex and the Brain," *USA Today,* July 8, 1991, p. 2A.

12. Ibid.

CHAPTER THREE
The Knower

1. Interview with a **Knower** brainstyle individual who was a controller in a manufacturing company, 1990.

2. *Fortune* "America's Toughest Bosses," February 27, 1989. p. 40.

3. Ibid.

CHAPTER FOUR
The Conceptor

1. Michael Meyer, *The Alexander Complex, The Dreams That Drive The Great Businessmen*, (Times Books, 1989) p. 29.

2. Ibid., p. 30.

3. Ibid., p. 19.

4. *Inc.,* "Reconcilable Differences," April 1991, pp. 78-87.

5. The Dallas Morning News, Business Section, May 3, 1992

6. Meyer, p. 34.

7. As quoted in Meyer, p. 202.

8. Meyer, p. 147.

9. Meyer, Ch. 8.

CHAPTER FIVE
The Conciliator

1. Howard Gardner, *Frames of Mind,* (Basic Books 1985.)

CHAPTER SIX
The Deliberator

1. Professor Hurt's initial findings showed that measures of brainstyle were statistically predictable for the 180 people tested in the following ways: The higher the organizational role, the more frequently the executive scored as a **Deliberator** brainstyle. There was also a correlation between salary and brainstyle, with more of those scoring as **Deliberators** earning higher salaries, supporting the previous finding.

2. As quoted in *Inc.,* "Thriving On Order," December 1989.

3. Tom Peters, *Thriving on Chaos,* (Harper Perennial Press, 1988).

4. Michael Meyer, *The Alexander Complex, The Dreams That Drive*

The Great Businessmen, (Times Books, 1989) p. 164.

5. Ibid., p. 164.

6. *Fortune* "America's Toughest Bosses," February 27, 1989. p. 40.

CHAPTER SEVEN
There Are No Bad BrainStyles, Only Bad Fits

1. Studies were conducted by: Granovetter, 1974; Helgensen, 1985; Smith, 1983; Stark, 1985.

2. *1990 Annual: Developing Human Resources,* "Networking Skills Inventory," (University Associates Press) pp. 153-156.

3. Ibid.

4. Ibid., Research on networking and influence were conducted in studies carried out by these professors.

5. *Fortune,* "America's Toughest Bosses," February 27, 1989, pp. 40-50.

6. Elek J. Ludvigh, III and Deborah Happ, "Extraversion and Preferred Level of Sensory Stimulation" pp. 359-365.

7. Richard Pascale, *Managing On the Edge,* (Simon and Schuster 1990).

CHAPTER EIGHT
Where You Can Take Your BrainStyle

1. R. Restak, M.D., "How to Outsmart Your Brain," *Self Magazine,*

March 1992, pp.108-109, The full quote is as follows:

"At UCLA researchers used PET scanning — an imaging procedure that can help trace brain functions — to compare the performance of people who scored very well on IQ tests with that of individuals scoring only within an average range. The researchers started off with the seemingly reasonable idea that 'smarter brains' work harder, generate more energy and consume more glucose.

Like light bulbs, the brains of 'bright' people were expected to illuminate more intensely than those of 'dimwits' with reduced wattage. The results showed just the opposite: Those who performed best on the IQ test tended, on average, to produce 'cooler,' more subdued PET scan patterns (blue and green colors), while their less intellectually gifted counterparts lit up like miniature Christmas trees ('hot' red and various orange hues). The brain of the less intelligent person seemed to have to work harder to achieve less.

Such biological constraints on human intelligence offend some people, who find it difficult to accept the idea that nature could apportion giftedness the same way as it does, say, beauty. But autopsies performed on the brains of extraordinarily gifted people demonstrate striking neurological differences from the average."

2. Ned Herrmann, *The Creative Brain*, (Brain Books, 1988).

3. Ned Herrmann, presentation to the American Creativity Association, May 1, 1992, Dallas, Texas.

4. Jerry White and John Welsh, *The Entrepreneur's Master Planning Guide,* (Prentice Hall Press, 1983).

5. <u>Ibid</u>., pp. 41-47.

6. Peter B. Vaill, "Towards a Behavioral Description of High-Performing Systems," George Washington University, Washington, DC. 1975, revised 1977.

7. *Inc.*, "The Truth About Start-Ups," April, 1991, p. 54.

8. Noel Tichy and Ram Charan, "Speed, Simplicity and Self-Confidence," *Harvard Business Review,* September, 1989.

9. <u>Ibid</u>.

10. Chapter Four, "Creating a Vision of Greatness: The First Step Toward Empowerment" in *The Empowered Manager,* Peter Block, Josey-Bass, 1987.

11. Pascale, p. 261.

12. <u>Ibid</u>.

13. *Fortune*, "The Bureaucracy Busters," June 17, 1991, pp. 36-50.

14. Brightman and Verhoeven, "Why Managerial Problem-Solving Groups Fail," *Business Magazine*, Jan - Mar, 1986 "Running Successful Problem-Solving Groups" <u>Ibid</u>., Apr - June, 1986.

15. *Inc.*, "The Truth About Start-Ups," April, 1991, p. 67.

16. <u>Ibid</u>., p. 54.

APPENDIX A
BrainStyles Background

1. Eric Berne, *Games People Play*, (Ballantine Books, 1964).

2. *Psychology*, Roediger, Rushton, Capaldi, Paris (Little, Brown & Co., 1987), Ch. 1.

3. Isabel Briggs Myers with Peter B. Myers, *Gifts Differing*, (Consulting Psychologists Press, 1980), p. 189.

4. Ibid., p. 189.

5. Ibid.

6. David Merrill, *Personal Styles and Effective Performance: Make Your Style Work for You*, (Radnor, Pa.: Chilton, 1981).

7. Robert Bolton and Dorothy Grover Bolton, *Social Style/Management Style*, (Amacom, 1984), p. 24.

8. Ibid., p. 5.

9. Ibid., p. 7.

10. Ibid., p. 8.

11. Isabel Briggs Myers with Peter B. Myers, *Gifts Differing*, (Consulting Psychologists Press, 1980), p. 12.

12. *Science News*, "Insight proves key to marital therapy", February 23, 1991, p. 118.

13. Emmy E. Werner, Ph.D., "High-Risk Children in Young Adulthood: A Longitudinal Study from Birth to 32 Years", Based

on a paper presented at the 1988 annual meeting of the American Orthopsychiatric Association in San Francisco. The author is at the University of California, Davis., p. 73.

14. David T. Lykken, University of Minnesota, Presidential Address to the Society of Psychophysiological Research, 1981, "Research With Twins: The Concept of Emergenesis," p. 371.

15. Ibid., p. 370.

16. Ibid., p. 364.

17. Robert Plomin and Judy Dunn, *In Health,* a magazine section of *People,* October, 1991.

18. *Fortune,* "The Inside Story of the Brain," December 3, 1990, pp. 87-100.

19. Robert Ornstein, *Multimind,* (Doubleday, 1986), p. 73.

20. Interview with Dr. Brandt, June, 1990.

21. Howard Gardner, *Frames of Mind, The Theory of Multiple Intelligences*, (Basic Books, 1983).

22. Dr. Wagner, *Practical Intelligence*, (Cambridge University Press, 1988).

23. Gary Lynch, as quoted in "The Infinite Voyage: Fires of the Mind" television documentary produced by QED Communications, Pittsburgh, PA., 1991.

24. Ned Herrmann, *"The Creative Brain"*, (Brain Books, 1988), as quoted in the *Training and Development Journal*, 1981.

25. Ibid.